Nico   2001

To our aspiring young "Actor"!
We are very proud of you.
    Love always,
    A.Angela, U.Danny, Christian and Andreas

D1466073

Katherine Mayfield has performed for over twenty years on stages across the country, and in film, television, and theater in New York City. Her favorite roles have included Annie Sullivan in *The Miracle Worker,* Rosalind in *As You Like It,* and Lucy in *You're a Good Man, Charlie Brown.* She has also appeared numerous times on the soap opera *Guiding Light.*

the
young
person's
guide to
a stage or
screen career

A C T I N G
A T O Z

katherine
mayfield

BACK STAGE BOOKS
An imprint of Watson-Guptill Publications
New York

*This book is dedicated to every young actor who has a dream,
and to the playful, creative child in all of us.*

Copyright © 1998, by Katherine Mayfield

Published in 1998 by Back Stage Books, an imprint of Watson-Guptill Publications, a division of BPI Communications, Inc., 1515 Broadway, New York, NY 10036-8986

Editor for Back Stage Books: Dale Ramsey
Book design: Bob Fillie, Graphiti Graphics, Inc.
Production manager: Ellen Greene

Library of Congress Cataloging-in-Publication Data for this title can be obtained by writing to the Library of Congress, Washington, D.C. 20540

ISBN 0-8230-8801-4

Manufactured in the United States of America
2 3 4 5 6 7 8 9 / 03 02 01 00

Acknowledgments

My DEEPEST APPRECIATION goes to the young actors who kindly shared their feelings, hopes, and dreams so that young actors everywhere would have a deeper understanding of acting: Justin Constantine, Patrick Link, Braden LuBell, Lindsay Riber, Jaime Nicole Rinne, Sarah Taylor, and Elizabeth Wetmore. I wish you all the success and happiness you hope for.

Special thanks are due to Andrew Wetmore, who helped me shape the book into a form that is user-friendly for kids; to Sam Rush of the Smith College Theater Department, Stan Sherer, and Jim Gipe for granting permission to use illustrations; to Elizabeth Wetmore for the use of her résumé; to my parents for their support and encouragement; to Bob Fillie for his eye-catching design; to Jean Atcheson for her excellent proofing help; and to my editor, Dale Ramsey, who always seems to know what I'm really trying to say, and whose patient and wise counsel guided me from beginning to end.

Contents

Introduction

SO YOU WANT TO BE AN ACTOR! Whether you've already done a lot of acting, or you're only starting to think about becoming one, this book can help you. The more you read, the more you'll learn about acting—all the way from A to Z.

This book will show you what it's *really* like to try to make your living as an actor. Then you can decide whether you'll choose acting as a career. If you do decide to be a professional actor, this book will help you get started. It will give you advice about how to find work, and teach you how to take care of yourself.

If you want to be an actor, you should do it because you love it more than anything else. If it makes you happy to perform, you'll be more successful than if you only want to be a star. There are many different ways to be an actor, professional or not. You'll learn all about them as you read the book.

However you do it, acting is fun. And whether you act to pursue a career on the stage, in film, and on television, or act simply for pleasure, I wish you lots of luck and good times!

KATHERINE MAYFIELD

Acting:
An Overview

WELCOME TO THE WORLD OF ACTING! It's a world of self-expression and creativity. It can be exciting to rehearse and perform a new play. Actors explore characters and their relationships onstage in front of hundreds of people. They go to opening and closing night parties and meet talented, interesting people. Being a professional actor also involves lots of hard work: training and studying, going to auditions and interviews, competing with hundreds of other actors for a role, and keeping yourself in good shape.

Many actors study for several years before they set out to become professionals—that is, to find jobs and make their living as actors. And even those actors who have gone through a training program and are already in the profession spend time each week improving their skills, polishing their talent, and keeping up with new plays and events in the world of show business. Pursuing a career as an actor means excitement, new experiences, and hard work.

Let's look at seven different fields in which you might find jobs as a professional actor.

THEATER

Live theater is the most basic and traditional way for an actor to practice his or her craft. When an actor is cast in a play, he'll usually spend four to six weeks rehearsing with the director and the other actors. Opening night is a big event, when the actors usually do the play in front of an audience for the first time. For many plays there are *previews,* when the play is performed for an audience a number of times before it officially opens. This permits the actors to see how audiences will respond to their work. Previews also give actors a chance to get comfortable in front of an audience before theater critics write their reviews of the show.

Most actors are trained by performing in the theater rather than by learning film or commercial skills. Working in front of an audience is a basic and necessary part of an actor's training, even if he or she later moves into film or television. And some actors who become film stars still return to the stage during their careers. They believe that the stage offers a rich experience for the actor that can be missing from film work.

New York is a major theater center, and Los Angeles and Chicago have many theater opportunities as well. In New York, new plays are first produced in Broadway and off-Broadway theaters. (Broadway is the main avenue in New York's theater district.) Most of the productions on Broadway are musicals. Off-Broadway theaters present more classics and new nonmusical (or "straight") comedies and dramas.

Many years ago, Broadway was the most important area for theater in the country. But over the years it has become more and more commercial, which means that the majority of the producers are trying to put on shows that will dazzle audiences and become instant hits. When these very commercial shows are created, most of the work that is done aims at giving the producer the best chance of making enormous profits. Some people believe that, as a result, the variety of productions has lessened over the years. Sometimes the quality of the show may be affected.

Many of the actors who land the best roles in professional theater have already made a

TALKING ABOUT ACTING

I asked one young actor: Do you plan to pursue a career as an actor after high school or college?

Meg, age 13: *I don't really want to be a professional actor, because it's such a competitive field. I'm not really cut out for that kind of thing. Acting is fun if you don't have to worry: "If I don't get this part, I can't pay my rent." It takes all the fun out of it.*

It's good to know exactly what you want to get from acting. Once you know that, you can decide whether to pursue it as your profession, or do some acting on a different level while you have another career. If you like acting because it's fun, then it will be fun for you anywhere you do it. If you don't like competing against others, then an acting career would probably be unpleasant for you. But if you want a professional career, then go for it. Just do some thinking about what you really want from it, and that will help you make the right decision.

name for themselves in film or television. It's hardest of all for a new actor to "break in" on Broadway.

But the quality and amount of theater produced in most other places has grown. There is probably a community theater near your home where you can take part in productions and try out for many different parts. In local theater, you can sharpen your skills and build up your list of credits. Many community theaters choose excellent, well-known shows, and have very talented people involved in putting them on.

FILM

Film acting is different from acting on the stage in a number of ways. Though the basic skills of acting are the same, the actor's performance in a film must be more limited, or "pulled back," in style. On the stage of a theater, an actor's gestures and expressions must be large enough to "fill the house," so that every member of the audience, even those in the last rows and top balconies, can see and hear the action. But in film acting, the camera magnifies every move the actors make, so they need to control their voice and gestures. On film, if you move your head even slightly to the side, or clench your jaw, the camera will pick up and magnify the movement. If you plan on doing any film work as an actor, you'll need to take some classes in "on-camera" performance, as well as in theater and acting training.

Another major difference between working in theater and in film is that, in theater, you rehearse the entire show for a period of time, and then perform the entire show over and over each night that the production runs. But in filming a movie, you may work on the final scenes first, then shoot the middle of the film, and then do the opening scenes last. It takes a lot of concentration in film acting to remember what you did in other scenes—that is, you must focus your attention so that you can keep your work consistent through the film.

Unlike play production, the process of making a film or commercial usually begins early in the morning. The work day is long, and actors may be acting for only 15 or 20 minutes out of every hour. The rest of the time is spent waiting for the crew to set up scenery or lights. Actors are often asked to do the same scene over and over again with slight changes. Because of this, the film actor's concentration is different from the theater actor's: His or her focus needs to last over a longer period of

Take: A single scene in a film, commercial, or TV show, shot from beginning to end, is a take. When everything is ready for the shot, the stage manager holds a clapboard in front of the camera. On it is written the number of the take. He or she will say "Take 1" (or "Take 2" for the second filming of that scene, and so on), and snap shut the clapboard. The clap it makes as it is shut helps the editor match up the image on the film with the sounds on the soundtrack.

time on a film shoot. As an actor, you'll need to learn how to relax and save your energy between **takes** and then to deliver a full-energy performance on short notice.

COMMERCIALS

Commercials are the short "spots" that advertise products during television shows. Again, commercial acting is different from theater and film acting. The skills required are similar to those used in film acting, but the point of a commercial is to sell a product rather than to tell a story. It helps if you are a good salesperson as well as a good actor.

Commercials are designed to make viewers feel that, if they buy the product, they will have more fun or their life will be better in some way. So commercials usually promote good and happy feelings, rather than the conflict and struggle on which plays and films are generally based.

DAYTIME AND PRIME-TIME TELEVISION

Soap operas (daytime television dramas) and prime-time television shows require many of the same skills that film acting does. The major difference is that the stories are *serial,* or ongoing from one show to the next. That is, the story unfolds and develops over months or years as the program is broadcast. An actor needs to be able to sustain and expand his or her character over a long period of time.

Soaps: Soap operas are often called soaps, for short. Both terms refer to daytime television dramas. The term "soap opera" first came about because manufacturers advertised laundry soap on the shows' commercials.

Look: Many casting directors and agents tend to put actors into groups based on their appearance. This leads to a practice known as *type casting.* As the term suggests, what *type* an actor appears to be is part of what lands him or her the job. The young mom, the doctor, the tough guy—these are familiar types that actors play again and again—if they have the look.

As unfair as it may seem, an actor's **look** is very important in most television work. You may want to watch some soaps or prime-time programs to see if you think your physical appearance would fit in on those shows. Even on comedy shows, most of the actors are attractive. Of course, their comedy skills are highly developed also. If you're interested in getting work on comedy shows, a class in

improvisation can be helpful. (Improv classes can be a lot of fun, and very useful for actors in any field.)

It will help you to watch other actors and the roles they play, so that you can see the different looks and types. Most casting directors will not cast "against type." If the role calls for a tall, muscular 32-year-old, they won't select an average-height, thin 21-year-old. Understanding this can save actors from making wasted efforts to get roles.

....
Improvisation: In an improvisation (or *improv*), two or more actors act out a short scene without knowing how it will go. They are given a theme or situation to begin, and they make up the words and actions as they go along. Improvisation helps actors learn to be creative.

REGIONAL AND SUMMER THEATER

Regional and summer theaters are similar to each other because the actor usually has to move to where the job is. There are theaters in just about every region of the country in big cities and small towns. A few of them will provide low-cost or no-cost housing when you work for them, but in many cases you'll have to find a place to stay yourself.

Regional theaters usually employ actors for a season (September through May) or longer. Sometimes they use local actors for small roles. If there is a regional theater in your city or town, you might wish to call and ask if you can submit your photo and résumé (these are topics we'll discuss later on). Another possibility is to find out if they offer classes for children or teens. This can be a good way to become involved in their productions.

Many of the plays or musicals that are produced at regional and summer theaters are "classics"—shows that have been performed over and over again through the years. (On page 107 is a suggested "Thirty-five Plays to Be Familiar With"). Plays that have recently been successful on Broadway and off-Broadway are usually included in the season. And some new plays also receive their very first productions—or *premieres*—in these theaters.

Regional and summer theaters offer actors a chance to perform in a number of different well-crafted plays and to work in a variety of styles. They can develop their skills and talent in different ways.

In summer theaters (also known as *summer stock*), productions are often musicals and comedies. The pace of putting productions together is *fast:* Each show may have only one week to rehearse before opening. At some theaters, the shows go up in **repertory,** with a new show open-

Photo by Jim Gipe

Repertory: At repertory theaters, several shows are chosen for the season. The actors rehearse the first show, and then begin performing it in the evenings while they rehearse the second show during the day. Then the second show will be added to the evening performances. Rehearsals for the third show begin during the day. There are plenty of stories about repertory theater actors who put on the wrong costume for the play that night, so save some space in your memory to keep track of the shows.

Some summer stock companies perform in outdoor theaters.

ing each week. Because of this, summer stock will be excellent training for you as an actor. You will learn very quickly how to put a show together and make it work.

INDUSTRIALS

The *industrial* is a type of show or training film that businesses produce for their employees. Perhaps they want to train machine operators to do their work safely, so they show them a short film about safety on the job.

Or a company might put together a video to welcome new employees and teach them certain guidelines they should follow. Or they may use a stage show to introduce their new products or services to their sales people and inspire them to sell it forcefully.

Industrials are produced for the business world and offer information rather than simply telling a story, so an actor who pursues industrial work needs to project a business-like image. If the world of business interests you, or if you look like a business person, industrials might be a good area for you to earn some of your income.

VOICE-OVERS

A voice-over is a job that pays you for the use of your voice. Believe it or not, this can be a strong career choice when it comes to making a good income as an actor. For that reason, the field is hard to break into. In voice-over work, the actor's voice is recorded for use on radio commercials; on television commercials in which you don't see the actor but only hear his or her voice; and for the voices of cartoon characters on TV and in movies.

On most commercials the voice-over work is done by men rather than women, but women are finding more chances to work in this field. If you want to work in voice-overs, you'll need to have a very well-trained voice—one of the necessary tools of the actor which we will explore in the next chapter. You'll also need to prepare a cassette tape of your voice doing commercials or character voices. It's best to have this recording made by a professional.

OTHER POSSIBILITIES

There are many other ways in which actors use their talents: performing on cruise ships and at theme parks, teaching at summer theater camps, or portraying a particular character at a historical site. All these kinds of jobs require specific skills in addition to your basic acting ability. For instance, if you're playing a character at a historical site, you may not need to learn your part from a script. You'll more likely be asked to

WHAT IS DINNER THEATER?

In dinner theater, plays are performed while the patrons eat dinner, or just afterwards, and the meal is included in the ticket price. It's similar to summer stock, but it isn't limited to that season. The shows performed are usually well-known and have been very successful. Most often they are musicals and comedies. Sometimes a dinner theater will perform a show of its own design, often based on a theme or historical time period. Actors who are hired to perform in dinner theaters usually wait on tables before the show begins, as part of their contract.

improvise, as the character, for several hours in various situations.

If you're interested in some of these possibilities, your first step might be to talk to one of the actors who perform these jobs. You'll get a good idea of what the experience is really like.

EXPLORE!

Learn all you can about acting, no matter what area of acting you're interested in. Try to see how it works as a business as well as an art form. Go see as much theater and film as you can, and talk to actors about their experiences. If you live near a large city, try to arrange to tour the backstage area of a major theater, or a film studio. The more you can find out, the more successful you're likely to be as an actor.

In the next chapter, you'll find out about what basics you'll need in order to become a professional actor.

Basic Tools of the Actor

ACTING IS DIFFERENT FROM MOST OTHER ARTS because actors use their own bodies and voices, rather than tools such as paints or instruments, to create art. Painters may create something that they "see" in their imaginations, but they use tools that are outside themselves—canvas or paper and paint—to create the picture. A musician expresses talent, skill, and love of music through a musical instrument. But an actor expresses and creates art through the self.

Some actors make the mistake of thinking that if they don't need any other tools besides their own voices and bodies, they don't need any training—that they can just get up on a stage, and acting will come easily. But actors need just as much training as musicians or visual artists. There are skills and techniques that will help them become the best they can be.

YOUR PHYSICAL TOOLS

As an actor, your physical tools will be your body and voice, so you'll need to keep them in top condition. Only when you're in good shape can you express the character traits and shifts of feeling that are necessary for good acting. Also, some roles may demand a certain amount of physical ability. You might play a classical role where you have to do **fencing**, or you might ride a horse, swim, or fight in a film.

Fencing: In the historic past, gentlemen fought in wars or settled arguments by dueling with swords, or fencing. Some of Shakespeare's plays, such as *Hamlet*, include scenes in which the actors fence. In the last few decades, fencing has become popular as a sport in itself.

9

Actors often need the skill of fencing in performance of Shakespeare's plays.

Exercise should be a primary objective for you. If you're in your teens and you play a sport such as basketball or go dancing frequently, you may not need a specific exercise program. But as you get into your twenties, it will be helpful to your growth as an actor if you develop a physical program for yourself. For example, yoga, strength training, swimming, and martial arts are very good choices. Strength, flexibility, and stamina are very important, because the physical demands of different characters you'll play could cover a wide range. If you are interested in working in classical theater or in film, you'll need to be strong and ready to learn various physical techniques. Experiment a little, until you find a program that you enjoy, because that will help you stick to it. A program that gives you a strengthening workout and develops flexibility is best. Eating a healthy diet will also provide you with the energy and stamina you need.

Whether you plan an ongoing program or not, you need to **warm up** your body and voice before rehearsals and performances. You need to have a good supply of energy onstage and be able to keep your focus throughout a rehearsal or performance, and if your body and voice are warmed up, it's easier to sustain your energy and express your character in a detailed way.

Warm up: This is the process of exercising your body and voice so that you're relaxed and energetic when you get onstage.

Most actors do stretching exercises, such as the following:

- Bending over at the waist and letting the head and arms dangle, then curling up slowly.

- Stretching the arms and legs gently.

- Moving the head around slowly so that your neck and shoulders relax.

The purpose of the warm-up is to get blood moving more rapidly through your body, and to relax the tense places. You don't need a full-scale heavy-duty exercise period. Some actors prefer to lie on the floor in a relaxed position and move their limbs gently.

When warming up, always remember to breathe fully and deeply, in and out.

Vocal training is as important as physical training. If your voice is not well trained, strain can result. Over a period of time, strain can cause real problems with your voice. Some performers, particularly those who work

If your role calls for a great deal of physical action, it's important to do a good warm-up.

in musical theater, have had major throat and voice problems because their voices were not properly trained. If you are planning on attending a college or other advanced theater program, vocal and physical training will be included in your classes. If you are planning on studying privately with an acting teacher instead, get his or her advice on voice exercises or on seeing a vocal coach.

You'll also need to learn how to warm up your voice. You can begin by humming quietly, and then working your way up to doing musical scales—sliding your voice up and down. This should not be done with tension, but rather as a way to get energy into your voice and get your breathing going. Many actors also do tongue twisters, such as "Peter Piper picked a peck of pickled peppers." Doing these exercises helps the lips, teeth, and tongue to get warmed up. Then the words you speak will come out more clearly. Just about anyone who directs plays at your school or in your town can suggest some good voice warm-up exercises.

Your voice, as well as your body, needs to be flexible and strong. It's important to develop a wide range in your voice, so that you can create characters with different vocal styles. Some characters may speak in high voices that seem to be centered in their noses—these are called nasal

Project: As an actor you must be able to throw—or project—the sound of your voice so that you are heard even in the back rows of the theater. It doesn't simply mean that you speak louder, though that is part of the skill. Projecting does not mean yelling. It's more like taking the energy you use in a conversation and magnifying it ten times to fill the space in a theater.

voices. Others will express themselves in deeper, rounded tones that are centered in the throat and chest. To be able to **project** your voice in a theater performance, you need all the vocal strength you can develop.

Most large theaters nowadays have excellent sound systems, and actors are wired with microphones so that they can be heard better. But projecting is still a necessary skill for an actor. It would be too bad to miss getting a big part in an outdoor production of a play, for instance, because nobody could hear you. In being heard, you also need to speak clearly and use your face and body so that the physical image you create supports the meaning of the words you're speaking.

As you probably know already, using tobacco, alcohol, or drugs will do more damage to your voice and body than give pleasure. And using them to try to improve your image does more harm to you than good. It's best to avoid them.

USING YOUR MIND

An understanding of people, their attitudes and beliefs, is essential to an actor's grasp of character and plot. If you don't feel you have this kind of understanding, you can learn to develop it by observing people closely. Watch how different people behave, and listen to the kinds of things they say. Begin to "train your brain" to think in terms of people's motives and actions. Ask yourself why someone in a dramatic situation speaks or acts a certain way. How might that person behave in a different situation? How might *you* behave if you were in that person's place? This kind of analysis will give you "people knowledge" that will be very valuable to you as an actor.

If you've decided to go to college, think about taking one or two psychology courses. Having a knowledge of how the human mind works can help you in creating characters.

As you develop your mind in this way, and learn to create and explore different characters, it's important to trust the ideas that you come up with. It may not turn out that every single idea you have about your character or the show will be brilliant, but many of your ideas probably will be right on target. So develop your instincts, and then believe in them.

As an actor learning and rehearsing a role, it will always be best to allow yourself to come up with lots of ideas. Then you can experiment with them, and discard the ones that don't work. This approach is much better than working with a lack of faith in your own intelligence. You don't want to develop the character you're playing only one or two steps in one direction. It's more exciting and skillful to be as creative as you can.

If you give your mind the freedom to pop up with unexpected ideas and possibilities, with a little practice it will do exactly that. And the more you give yourself room to be creative, the more creative you'll become. Some actors with limited ideas about how a character should be expressed cut themselves off from a new angle on the character and the show. They may even miss the deeper meaning of the story. Most theater productions and films, after all, hold a mirror up to the world and deepen our understanding of all human life. Casting directors and agents, as well as audience members, often enjoy and remember a performance that went beyond what they expected—a performance that was more interesting than most of the others they've seen.

This does not mean that you should try to be weird or unusual just to get attention. Most actors who try to get noticed by being strange are not very successful in pursuing a career. With your director's help, you'll be able to make some inventive choices about how to play the character, choices that are within the natural bounds of what the character in that script would actually do. Your goal is to bring the play to life and to make the best possible version of the script unfold before the audience. You want to bring as much of the variety of human nature to the role as you can, not to be as weird as possible. With that in mind, encourage your creativity, and trust your body to express it in unusual and interesting ways.

YOUR SOUL OR SPIRIT

Most audience members go to the theater or to a film to be emotionally touched in some way: to be thrilled or excited, to be moved to tears or laughter, and to feel a bond with other people. One of the most important aspects of your work as an

TALKING ABOUT ACTING

I asked one young actor: What do you want from an acting career?

Liz, age 17: *Doing what I love, and having that be my mode of living, would be the best thing in the world. And if I just happen to run into fame and fortune on the way, that's fine with me.*

This is a pretty sensible outlook. Most actors are more successful when their goal is "to be a working actor" rather than "to be a star." And being a working actor is a much more realistic goal. The odds are more in your favor.

actor is to learn to connect with others from your inner self—your soul, or spirit, or "center." By doing this, you can make others more aware of how they take part in the experience of being human.

There are many different forms of training for this aspect of acting. Yoga and martial arts, Reiki and meditation help some people to relax and deepen their connection to their inner self on their own. Some people need a teacher. In searching for a method that works for you, you'll need to trust your instincts. If you've begun studying martial arts, and you realize that it's something you're just not attracted to, try something else instead. If meditation fascinates you, and you find yourself eager to learn about different techniques and ideas, then that's probably a good match for you. You'll just know when you've found a teacher, or an idea, or a program that's right for you.

When you find something you like, investigate as many different parts of it as you can. Working on your inner self will not only increase your enjoyment of acting and your ability to act, it will help you to live a richer life as well.

Career Issues

Now that you've read about the different fields in acting and the basic tools that an actor needs, you may be wondering if you really can have an acting career. What are the issues involved? What are the realities you'll have to deal with? Are you cut out to be an actor?

First of all, anyone can be an actor. There are many, many theaters in every part of the world, and you can always find a way to enjoy acting. However, some people are better *suited to the profession* than others are. Think about these issues for a moment:

- Are you uncomfortable with the idea that you may try out for fifty roles before you get one?

- Do you dislike the possibility that you might start out by playing tiny roles with no lines?

- Does it bother you that someone with less talent and personality than you may be more successful than you?

- Could you have difficulty working at a career while struggling to pay your bills for five or ten years—or longer?

If your answers to these questions are mostly *yes*, you need to think twice about becoming a professional actor. The world of acting is full of excitement. But you do work hard for the thrill of playing a role in front of a camera or a live audience, for the fun of working with others who share the same love of theater, TV, and movies that you do. There are also some sacrifices to be made.

THE REALITY OF AN ACTING CAREER

Many people believe that acting is very easy. All you have to do, they think, is learn the lines and the movements, then get up in front of the audience or the camera, have fun, and become famous. But there's much more to it.

We've already talked about the work you must do to have a clear, well-trained voice so everyone in the audience will be able to understand you. We've seen that you'll need to keep your body flexible so that you can express all kinds of thoughts and feelings.

Also, you'll need to learn how to **audition,** how to create a character, how to work with a director and other actors, and how to promote yourself if you choose to pursue a career. Perhaps most important, you need to know how to deal with certain difficulties. You need to learn how to handle the unhappy feeling of being turned down for a part you wanted. You need to know how to keep your spirits up when you're not working on a role. You must be able to deal carefully with others in the business end of acting who may not care about what will truly benefit you.

Audition: In an audition, you try out for a role by presenting a memorized speech or reading a scene from a script with other actors.

Yes, you *can* be an actor. What you need to do first is find out what kinds of preparation are necessary. You'll definitely need several years of basic training as an actor. It will also help you to sharpen your skills as you go along, by taking classes fairly often.

When you hear or read about the lives of famous actors, you don't usually learn about the realities of their lives and the work they do. Here are a few things you need to know in order to make a smart career decision:

• Most acting careers require a lot of hard work, day in and day out, over a long period of time. For some actors it takes ten years or more to achieve much success. Even after years of effort, training and promoting yourself, your career may not be as successful as you'd like. And it can often seem that there's no particular reason why one actor makes it and another doesn't. This can make the business seem very unfair.

• Though you'll enjoy the times you're rehearsing and performing, there may often be a long wait between jobs.

• Numerous agents, casting directors, directors, and producers will not be interested in you as an actor unless you've already earned some amount of fame. They like to know that someone else is already interested in you before they call you in for an audition or an interview. This is why actors who land a good job will often shortly get another, and another—sometimes several in a row. People don't seem to trust their own opinions about you as much as they trust the opinions of others.

• Often the focus of people such as agents, casting directors, and studio executives is on making money rather than on helping you or being artistic.

• You'll need to support yourself with food and shelter, and you'll also have the added expenses of pursuing an acting career—and that can cost a lot of money. An actor's photo session can cost from $300 to $1,000, and fees to join a union are close to $1,000 for the first payment. And there are all the classes to pay for, and clothing and grooming expenses. For instance, you'll want a hair style that makes you look your best.

• You may have to work with some people that you don't like very much. Television and magazines tend to glamourize famous actors, making them all look and sound wonderful. Many of them really are wonderful, but actors are human beings, after all. Some are hard to work with, some may not be helpful to their fellow actors, some will be rude to you, and so on.

• The media portrays most stars as "having it all," but in reality they have problems and fears like everyone else. In fact, once an actor achieves some fame, he or she is under tremendous pressure to stay famous. There are always younger, talented actors moving onto the scene. Some stars have become anxious or depressed enough to start using alcohol or drugs as a way to escape the pressure—with bad results.

It can be difficult to face the realities of an acting career. But it's better to know before you start how difficult it can be. You might decide you'd

I asked one young actor: What's your favorite thing about acting?

Patrick, age 12: *I like to be the center of attention—the guy that everyone else is watching. You can get away from all the things that are happening in school and in your life, and be happy for a while.*

Getting away from your problems for a while can help you deal with stress in your life. But don't go too far with this idea, or you'll begin trying to ignore your problems, hoping they'll just go away while you're acting. This can be an easy trap for actors to fall into. If you try to live only for the moments you can act, your problems can get more stressful.

rather spend your time and money doing something else that you love almost as much. You might decide that you can deal with the problems, as many actors do. You might even find the challenges exciting and energizing.

OTHER POSSIBILITIES

One thing you might want to consider is to get training in a field that is more stable and financially secure than acting. You could pursue your acting dreams on a local level, with an amateur theater group in your community, but you would have a steady income from working at a job that you also have an interest in.

In that case, you'd probably get to play more of the roles you want to play, because once you get known in a local theater, they'll usually call you again and again. Sometimes you can help choose plays that have roles you'd like to do. You might have more control in this kind of amateur situation. In a professional career, unless you are very well known, you'll usually have little say about the chances you'll get to play your favorite kinds of roles.

Many actors have started a local theater company with the idea of performing in plays they choose. This is a good alternative to pursuing a career as a professional.

Whatever you choose to do with your life, your life is your own to create, not anyone else's. The most important thing is to choose what makes you happy, and you're the only one who can figure out what that is. And even if you take a long time to decide about acting, that's fine—take some time to think it over. You can always change your mind, no matter what you choose.

Now take a deep breath, and next we'll find out what a day in the life of an actor is like.

A **D**ay in the Life of an Actor

MARK IS AN ACTOR who has lived in New York City for five years. Born and raised in a suburb of Cincinnati, Ohio, he graduated from the theater training program at Northwestern University. Then he moved to New York. At first, he had some difficulty adjusting to life in a large city. The noise and the great numbers of people were hard to take. And he had the feeling that he had to "keep up" with everything. In the last two years, though, Mark has become more comfortable living and working in a big city.

Mark actually lives in Brooklyn, one of the boroughs (sections) of New York City, in a neighborhood called Park Slope. He has to spend 40 minutes in the morning and in the evening riding the subway to and from Manhattan. Park Slope is quieter and somewhat safer than many Manhattan neighborhoods, and it costs him less to rent an apartment there. Mark needs to live in an area that isn't too expensive because he's working part-time rather than full-time so he can pursue his acting career.

Let's follow Mark around on one day in his life as an actor.

MORNING

Mark gets up around 7:30 A.M. and goes running in the park to keep his body fit, flexible, and healthy. After he showers and eats breakfast, he gets on the subway for an audition with a casting director at 10 A.M. He gets to the casting director's office a few minutes before his appointment, and notices that the office is busy. There are three other actors already waiting, the phone is ringing, and an assistant is opening and sorting the mail.

Mark waits about 20 minutes to see the casting director, humming softly to warm up his voice. When his name is called, he walks into the inner office. The casting director is on the phone, but she waves him into a seat. After a few more words, she hangs up the phone and speaks briefly to Mark, asking about his training and experience. Then she gives him a script, tells him what role she'd like him to read, and makes another phone call while Mark looks at the script.

After a moment Mark gets some ideas about his role in the script. He knows he has to make a quick choice about how to put across the character he's going to play for a few minutes there in the casting director's office. When the casting director gets off the phone, she tells him to go ahead. Mark reads the scene aloud for her. The casting director thanks him and says, "We'll let you know." After a hurried lunch Mark is off to his **day job,** working as a service person for a caterer.

Day job: The work actors do for money to live on while they're pursuing acting work.

AFTERNOON

Mark works for the caterer at a lunchtime meeting for business executives until 3:30 P.M. Then he rides the subway across town to a photographer's studio. There he picks up his contact sheets, which show him many small versions of photos taken of him in a recent photo session (See "Contact sheets," page 90.). After looking them over for a few minutes, he marks a few he thinks will be good choices for a larger final photo.

Mark then stops at a pay phone to call his voice mail and returns a call to a casting director who wants to know if he's available for work the next day. He stops for dinner at a health food restaurant, and gets on the subway to go uptown to audition for a role in an off-off-Broadway play.

Mark doesn't particularly like the script for this play, but he thinks the director is talented, and Mark would like to work with him. He arrives at the small theater (it has only 80 seats). The auditions are running late, and though his appointment was for 6:30 P.M., it's almost 8 before he gets to do his **monologue.** The audition doesn't go as well as Mark wanted it to because he's tired. But he's happy he got to meet the director.

Monologue: This is the actor's term for a speech you prepare to perform by yourself in an audition.

EVENING

On the way back to the subway, Mark picks up a copy of *Back Stage,* the New York weekly theater newspaper. While he rides the subway home, he looks through the casting notices. These are small ads published in the paper that tell him:

- What is being cast (play, film, commercial, and so on)

- What kinds of roles are available

- Who is casting (a theater company, a casting director, a film director)

- How to apply (send photo or attend audition)

When Mark gets home, he prepares three letters to send with his photo and résumé in response to the ads. (See "Résumés" on page 96.) The casting director he spoke to that afternoon had told him to report to the movie set at 7:30 to work as an extra. (See "Extra Work," on page 123.) He sets his alarm clock for 6 A.M., so he can be on time.

As you can see, a day in the life of an actor is a busy one. On other days, Mark might work with an acting coach on the monologues he prepares for his auditions. Or he might take a movement or voice class. He might go to see a friend in a show, send postcards to people in the business to keep them updated about his recent work, or go to a copy shop to get copies of his résumé.

On some Saturdays he spends a lot of time waiting in line to audition for a new play. Other times he gets up at 5:30 A.M. to wait several hours to sign up for an audition held by the actors' union, Actors' Equity.

Mark is excited by the variety and challenge of pursuing an acting career—that's what keeps him going. He likes being on the go and keeping in contact with a lot of talented people. He is lively and friendly, and that serves him well as he pursues his dream.

EVERYONE IS DIFFERENT

Mark's roommate, John, is also an actor. But he doesn't enjoy the hard work of pursuing his career as much as Mark does. He's shy compared to Mark, and so doesn't make friends with people as easily. The noise and the busy excitement of the city distract him. He feels more comfortable knowing ahead of time what he'll be doing for the next week. For this rea-

TALKING ABOUT ACTING

I asked a young actor I know: What do you think it would be like to be a professional actor?

Elizabeth, age 17: *Really, really hectic—a big roller coaster. It'd be frustrating not to have a stable job, unless you're cast in a long-running Broadway show. But that's the thrill of the chase—finding a job and doing it well, seeing it through to the production, and then going on to the next one.*

The "thrill of the chase" does appeal to a lot of actors. And it is like a roller coaster. The only difference is that when you're on a roller coaster at an amusement park, you can get off and go home. When you're pursuing a career, the ride doesn't stop. It becomes part of your day-to-day life. It can make you feel there's no time to rest. You'll need to go, go, go—but let yourself step back once in a while and take time to relax!

son the constant changes, uncertain schedules, and hasty activities John is involved in as an actor are sometimes confusing and stressful for him.

Both John and Mark are perfectly normal people—they're just different from each other. No one would be able to predict which of them might have success as an actor. Both of them are talented, both of them may become wonderful actors. But Mark will probably be more comfortable pursuing his career than John will, simply because he enjoys the process.

If you have the same goals as Mark and John, it's important to understand yourself well enough to know whether or not you'll be able to face the actor's day-to-day realities.

TWO YOUNG ACTRESSES

In order to get another look at the picture, let's follow Marla and Terry, who share a small apartment in Los Angeles. Marla, who works part-time as a secretary for a fashion designer, is always on the go. She gets tense when she doesn't have anything to do. She's eager to go to every audition she can, even for projects that don't include a role she could play. She'll immediately start a conversation with anyone, to see if she can find out about other auditions or contact someone in the acting business. Sometimes people wish she would calm down a little.

Marla also mails her photos to everyone she possibly can, and calls casting directors and agents every week to let them know she's available for work. And she takes acting, dance, and voice classes several afternoons a week.

Terry is less talkative and less on-the-go than Marla. Still, she pursues her career steadily. She has determination. She stays in touch with people she has met whose work she respects, but she's careful not to pester them. She chooses auditions carefully, based on whether or not she thinks she's right for the role. She works hard on the material she will present in her auditions. That way she feels comfortable and confident when she auditions.

Terry shares information with her actor friends and tries to form relationships in show business with actors and directors whose work she believes is high-quality.

Terry and Marla each have their individual style of pursuing an acting career and dealing with other people. Both are talented and work hard. But Marla may quickly come to feel that it's all too much for her. She's made a habit of keeping in touch with so many people and going to so many auditions that after several years of frantic work, she may feel too tired to pursue an acting career any longer. She may move on to another field.

An actor with Terry's steady approach, who uses her energy more carefully, would probably be able to pursue a career for a longer time. That way, she'll increase her chances of success.

Before you make the decision to be an actor, it's important to think about how well your personality will blend with the day-to-day reality. Anyone can pursue an acting career, no matter what his or her personality is like. But some people are more suited to an actor's life-style than others. You can ask yourself some questions to get an idea of whether or not you'd feel comfortable living as an actor:

- Do you enjoy meeting people?

- Do you like having a variety of things to do?

- Do you like being on the go?

- Do you have steady work habits? Enough to keep up with the business side of acting, which is not as interesting as the acting itself?

- Do you try to keep yourself healthy?

- Are you comfortable with new and different situations?

If you answered yes to every question, you would probably enjoy the process of pursuing a career.

BEING WHO YOU ARE

There have been major stars who were actually on the shy side, such as Greta Garbo and James Dean. And just because an actor is shy doesn't mean that he or she won't be successful. But it helps to know ahead of time that it can be more difficult for an actor who is shy to pursue a career, because actors must spend a lot of time and energy meeting people and promoting themselves.

If you are shy, you might work on learning how to be more comfortable with meeting people. Push yourself a little: Try starting a conversation with someone you know but not very well. Express yourself around other people—for example, learn to show that you are proud of your accomplishments and are able to talk about them.

You don't need to try to be someone you're not. It's better to be yourself and not think you have to act or feel a certain way in order to impress people. People in the acting business would rather see you as you really are than meet someone who's putting on an act. Even though acting is a business in which image and personality play a major role, people are much more impressed with someone who is honest and real than they are by a phony.

An actor's life is exciting, but it can also be difficult, as we've seen. Every time an actor goes to an audition, he or she has a good chance of being rejected. The stories of actors that magazines such as *Teen* and *People* present usually don't show the reality behind the images of glamour. Even major stars have to work hard to keep informed about which roles are available, which projects they might want to do, and what kind of image the public has of them. Our society tends to raise the big actors to a high position—that's why they're called *stars*, after all. Their lives are made to look easy and fun, while the effort that led to their prestige stays hidden. You need to know ahead of time that the images you see of the lives of the stars are only part of the picture.

TALKING ABOUT ACTING

I asked: What do you think it would really be like to be a professional actor?

David, age 12: *I hear all these stories that some of my favorite actors tell in interviews about how long it took them to get their big breaks, and I really get scared. But if I do end up getting a big break, hopefully, after that it'll be more fun than hard.*

Your favorite actors are right! It can take ten, fifteen, even twenty years of steady work before you can make a living entirely from acting. By the time most actors have worked on their careers long enough to call it their full-time job, they're in their late 30s or early 40s. And most of them never get that "big break." Usually it takes talent and hard work. Being in the right place at the right time can bring you good luck, but the "big break" is pretty much a myth.

No one can predict who will be successful and who will not. There are very talented actors who didn't become successful, for no apparent reason at all. And some actors you see in big roles might seem to have very little talent. If you love acting more than anything else in the world, if performing makes you happier than anything else you do, then you should go ahead and pursue a career as an actor. Who knows what will happen?

But don't forget: Acting is just like any other business. It takes a lot of time and effort to lay the foundation and build steadily on it in order to succeed. And as we'll see in the pages ahead, it's often *more* of a business than an art form. In the next section, you'll learn some steps you can take to increase your chances of success in the acting business.

Everything You'll Need

Promote: This term refers to the things actors do to increase the chances that they'll get jobs on the stage, in films, and on TV. When a business begins to sell a product, it usually promotes it through marketing and advertising. When you promote yourself as an actor, you're advertising yourself as a professional, ready to do a role.

NOW THAT YOU HAVE A FEELING for what it's like to be a professional actor, it's time to show you a list of all the things a beginning actor needs. Some of these things are skills that you'll need to develop, and others are objects, such as photos and résumés, that will help you **promote** yourself as an actor.

Promoting yourself includes sending photos and résumés to casting directors and agents, and sending **flyers** about a show or film you're in to people in the business. Some actors put their photos in theatrical newspapers, or on the Internet at specific casting sites. You can look into these possibilities and decide for yourself whether they'll help you.

You can be creative in promoting yourself, but don't let your ideas get too weird. If you have an idea about promoting yourself, but aren't sure if it would work, ask for advice from a teacher or someone else that you trust. You always want what you do to look professional.

Promotion also includes having audition monologues that you've memorized and rehearsed many times so

Flyers: These are announcements, usually printed on one sheet of colored paper, of the performances of a play, the location of the theater, the dates and times of the show, and the cast. They are simple tools for promoting shows and the actors in them.

you're always ready if an audition comes up suddenly. Your monologue will need to be a whole speech which is not interrupted by other characters' lines. It's best to choose one from a less well-known play so that you're not using the same monologue that a lot of other actors are using. The main thing is to work on it just as much as you would for a role that you're cast in so that you do your best in auditions.

WORKING ON SKILLS

Some of the skills you'll need in order to become a professional actor include the basic tools mentioned under **B**: "Basic Tools of the Actor". Movement training or dance classes will give you a feeling of being comfortable in your body. In acting classes you'll learn to feel at ease onstage in front of people. And with vocal study, especially if your voice is soft, you'll get some training to project your voice and speak with expression.

You'll also need to learn how to memorize your lines. This is a skill that you can pick up in your own way, however you can do it best. Some people like to read their lines over and over in order to memorize them. Some study them silently without speaking them out loud. We'll say more about memorizing lines later (see page 47, "In Rehearsal").

If you'd like to perform in musicals, you'll need the skills of singing and dancing as well. Ask for advice on finding a good singing teacher. Some are very good, and a few are not. Do your best to study with someone people have a high opinion of. (You can ask your acting teacher, a director, or another actor who has a good voice.) For dance classes, you could start with either ballet or modern dance. You'll probably want to take some tap and jazz classes, too—the dances in most musicals are based on these styles. Ballroom dances, such as the waltz, can be good to know because they'll add a graceful quality to your movement. If you can learn to play any musical instruments—especially piano or guitar—you'll have a few more chances to be cast in certain kinds of shows.

Most of the productions on Broadway today are musicals, and it's unlikely that this will change in the near future. So even if you decide you'd rather do straight theater (without music), it still might be a good idea to learn to sing and dance fairly well. Any skill that increases the range of what you can do will increase your chances of being cast.

OTHER TOOLS YOU'LL NEED

As you probably know, the actor's main tools of promotion are his or her photo and résumé. The photo is normally black and white and is 8 inches wide and 10 inches high. The résumé, which lists the actor's experience and training, is stapled to the back of the photo. You can learn more about photos and résumés in the "Photos" and "Résumés" chapters later in the book.

You'll also need postcards—that is, a postcard-sized print of one or two of your photos, with your name and voice mail number printed at the bottom. With postcards, you can stay in contact with people in the business in a quick, easy way. You can let them know when you're involved in a project without having to send a photo and résumé every time—which could get very expensive. Both the photos and the postcards can be duplicated at a printing company which specializes in actors' photos—you can look in the Yellow Pages under Photographic Reproduction, or ask a photographer who specializes in actors' photos for advice.

As an actor, you'll be mailing your photo and résumé to casting directors, agents, and possibly directors and producers—the people who cast the roles or have access to casting information. You'll make lots of trips to the post office and spend quite a bit on stamps. This chapter is about *all* the things you'll need, so here are two more items every beginning actor has to pay serious attention to: writing paper and envelopes. They may not be exciting, but believe it or not, they're important! Good quality paper and envelopes will help you present a professional image.

Actors need to get a supply of 9-inch by 12-inch envelopes for sending photos and résumés. These are usually made of a yellowish stiff paper. If you have a large budget to play with, you can use colored envelopes—these come in cheerful colors such as blue, green, pink, and red. Some actors like to use them because they attract a little more attention than the plain ones when they show up in someone's mail. But they are more expensive than the regular envelopes. If you do choose colored envelopes, you're probably better off picking a color that's not too hard to take. If it's neon green or bright orange, you may turn some people off.

Another helpful item is a box of labels for addressing the envelopes. If you can type the names and addresses for the people you're mailing to, your envelopes will look more professional. You can also buy pre-printed labels at many theatrical bookstores.

Cover letter: A letter that introduces you and states the reason you're contacting the person. People in most fields send cover letters with their résumés when they inquire about a job. You'll need to send a cover letter when you mail your photo and résumé to a casting director or agent. (See page 100 for an example.)

You'll also need some 8½-inch by 11-inch paper to type your **cover letters** on. Your name, address, and telephone number should be printed at the top. (Paper that's specially printed for you is called *letterhead*.) You can have a printing company create your letterhead, or you can make it yourself if you have a computer.

Some kind of calendar will help you keep track of your audition appointments, rehearsals, and performances. The best kind to have is a pocket-sized one that you could carry around easily. And it should have enough room in every day to record several events. You might have three auditions in one day, an appointment with a photographer, and a rehearsal in the evening. Remember, you're going to be busy!

WHAT YOU'LL NEED TO READ

You can usually find listings of auditions in your area in the arts section of the local newspaper. If you live in a big city, there may be a weekly newspaper that covers only the arts. Ask at a good newsstand or at the library to find out about publications you would read as an actor. In New York, you'd read *Back Stage*, and in Los Angeles, you'd read *Back Stage West* and *Dramalogue*. If you're organized, every week you'll sit down with the newspaper and your calendar and write in the times and places of auditions you want to go to.

Other good references are the *Casting and Survival Guide*, and *Ross Reports*, a monthly listing of major television producers, TV shows, casting directors, and agents. There are also many other things for actors to read, plenty of books on acting technique and theater and show-business magazines full of fascinating articles.

You can also subscribe to the Stage & Screen Book Club, which is a service that allows you to order and receive current theater and film books by mail. You can write to them for information at this address:

Stage & Screen
6550 E. 30th Street
P.O. Box 6309
Indianapolis, IN 46206-6309

CLOTHING

Finally, you'll need a nice outfit or two to wear to auditions, and a pair of neat, clean-looking shoes. Actors need clothing and shoes that are comfortable. You may have to stand in line for long periods of time at an audition, and there's nothing worse than having your feet hurt or wishing you could just get out of your clothes. You want to have your mind on your acting and be relaxed and ready to do your best work—rather than thinking about how uncomfortable you are. See if you can get some professional advice about the colors and styles that look best on you. If you look and feel great, you'll not only get a good response, but you'll enjoy auditions more.

Now let's find out more about the people you'll want to meet: casting directors and agents.

Finding Out About Casting Directors and Agents

CASTING DIRECTORS AND AGENTS are professional show business people who find the actors needed for plays, films, television shows, and even commercials. You will want to stay in contact with them as your career progresses.

They are certainly key people, but actors need to remember an important point: Casting directors and agents do not see their job as helping actors to get their careers going. Instead, they are usually most interested in whether your look and your talent are exactly what *they* need to "market" you to producers and directors. If they think they can, they will do so in order to make their living.

Some actors believe that if they can get to know a top casting director or sign a contract with an agent, their career will progress steadily. But this is not the case. Both casting directors and agents are usually more interested in actors who have already made at least a small name for themselves in theater, film, or commercials.

This doesn't mean it's a waste of time to mail them your photo and résumé. It simply means that they may not contact you until you've had a small part in a major film or performed in a show off-off-Broadway. Casting directors and agents see so many actors that it takes a while before they're aware of who you are. The same way that it takes you some time to find out who they are and what they might be looking for, it takes them time to remember an actor's name and face.

But there is a good reason to stay in contact with casting directors and agents. One day, if you get to where you're doing regular work and you've kept in touch, they'll already be familiar with you. At that point, if a role comes along for which you're well suited, they'll probably give you a call.

CASTING DIRECTORS

When a director of a play or film is ready to cast the roles, he or she will often hire a casting director to suggest actors for at least some of the parts. Sometimes there are parts that are difficult to cast—such as a very short, very fat actor, or a person who can speak a certain foreign language. Casting directors save directors all the work of learning about a large variety of actors. Most directors make a point of seeing new shows and getting to know actors whose work they respect. But the talent pool of actors in any major city is so large that it's impossible for a director to keep track of every actor he or she might want to use. A casting director's job is to know which actors might be particularly good for a role.

The director sends the casting director a description of the characters that need to be cast. Then the casting director will call in several actors to audition before narrowing the list to just a few. Those actors will then have a **callback** to audition for the director. Casting directors are under tremendous time pressure, because they often have to complete the entire casting process in only a week or two. They may sometimes seem abrupt or rude to actors for that reason.

Callback: This term is used a great deal by actors. It means a second audition or interview for the same role. You usually audition in front of more people at the callback than at the first audition.

Let's say you're starting out as an actor. You want to introduce yourself to a casting director first by mail: You send him or her your photo and résumé, along with a flyer for a show you're in. If you've done some film work, you send a cover letter with your photo and résumé offering to mail in a videotape containing clips (scenes) of your film work. It's best not to send a videotape right off the bat without first asking if they will accept it. Again, casting directors are so busy that they may not have a chance to look at the tape, and it may get lost at their office. They may just throw it away if they don't know who you are. (We'll say more about videotapes on page 115.)

It's best to contact these people first by mail because most casting directors are so busy they won't like your dropping in without notice. If they've met you before, they might appreciate it, *maybe*, but generally they just don't have time to see every actor who might decide to stop by.

In your cover letter you briefly describe your training and experience. And you say that you'll call in about ten days to ask about coming in for an interview. Ten days leaves enough time between sending the letter and calling the office for the letter to arrive and get read.

When you call the office, be polite and not pushy. Ask if you might arrange a time to audition or to come in for an interview. If they tell you they're not seeing anyone at this time, ask when you might try again. Should you keep in touch with postcards?

Don't let the people you contact scare you when they sound a little grouchy. But also avoid being so pushy that they never want to hear from you again. Try to walk the fine line between keeping them aware of who you are and contacting them more than you need to.

AGENTS

The job of the agent is to schedule auditions for the actors who have made an agreement to pay them a portion of the money they make (a *commission*). These actors sign a written agreement, or *contract,* with the agent and are called the agent's *clients.*

The agent submits the photos of his or her clients to casting directors, producers, or directors for a chance at a particular role. Some agents give their clients advice on photos, and also on things like clothes to wear, good grooming, classes to take, and so on. Some are very good at giving support and encouragement to their clients.

However, most agents are extremely choosy about the actors they will take on as their clients. Generally, they are interested in actors who already have a number of items listed on their résumés which show that the actor has done interesting work in the past. These items, which are often called *credits,* show the agent that the actor is already well on the way to a successful career. (There's more about how you would write your own résumé on page 96.)

Some actors think that if they can get a good agent to represent them, they'll have it made and finally be able to relax. But an agent cannot get you a job. He or she can only arrange auditions and interviews for you. It will be up to you to get the job.

Again, let's say you're starting out as an actor. You contact agents the same way you contact casting directors: by mailing a photo and résumé, waiting about ten days, and calling to ask if you can set up an audition or interview. It's best to notify agents when you have a good role in a show, so you can send them a flyer two or three weeks ahead of time. One thing agents will do, when they have time, is come to see your work.

Like most people, agents and casting directors want to see good plays, as well as good work. They are not pleased if they come to a show that hasn't got much going for it. So you'll want to invite them only when you're sure the show is good—and only when you're doing work you're proud of.

Actors always need to be careful about business matters. They need to be on their guard when any agent charges a set fee or asks for money up front. Agents are supposed to make money only when the actor is paid for his or her work. Their commission is usually 10 to 15 percent of the actor's total payment.

WATCHING OUT FOR YOURSELF

Some agents will tell you that they charge a fee to put their clients' photos into books or on the Internet as a way to promote you to casting directors. Almost all of these kinds of excuses for charging you money are worthless. Many are invented to cheat actors. You can tell the agent you'd like to think about it, and if right away the agent pressures you to decide, you can be pretty sure something is not right. If an agent tries to sell you on the idea of a client photo book or website, ask to see it. You can often tell by looking at the client photos whether or not it's something that would benefit you. And if the agent doesn't have something to show you, you'd be smart to pass up the offer.

Another good idea is to ask around to see if other actors you know have heard anything about a particular agent.

Next, we'll learn about what it's like to go on an interview with an agent, and an audition with a casting director.

Going to Interviews and Auditions

IMAGINE YOU'RE A PROFESSIONAL ACTOR. You get home one day, and discover that you have a message on your voice mail that Ms. Smythe, a theatrical agent, wants you to come in for an interview. What do you do first? Run out and buy some new clothes? Brush up your favorite audition song? Let's look at what you would do as an actor with an important meeting ahead. You'll get a strong idea of what every actor goes through many times in a career. Here's what you could expect as an actor yourself and what you'd do to make the most of it.

You call Ms. Smythe to set up a time to audition. Try to be as flexible as you can—check your calendar before you get on the phone, and find several times when you could do it. You'd allow at least an hour for the interview, because the other people who came before you are sometimes late, so appointments may run behind. And you'd allow plenty of time for traveling to the office. Buses can often be late, and traffic slow!

A good actor knows how to be business-like and brief on the phone. You want to tell whoever answers that the agent left a message for you. That way, the person on the other end knows you're someone the agent wants to speak to. Don't chat about the weather or the latest news, unless the agent does so first. Remember, agents are busy people, and you want them to spend time with you in person rather than on the phone. Make sure you have the time and date of the interview noted correctly in your calendar.

It's a good idea to have a few monologues prepared for an occasion like this. Be ready to do a variety: Perhaps a comic monologue, and one that's more straight drama. If you do classical theater, like Shakespeare, have a classical monologue ready. If you sing, have a few different songs ready. You never know what an agent might ask you to do!

INTERVIEWING WITH AN AGENT

What do you wear to the interview? Clothes that look professional and feel comfortable. If you have a dress or a suit that people keep telling you looks great on you, wear that. Or wear your favorite piece of clothing, the one that always makes you feel special. You want to look good, but feel just right, so you'll be at your best.

Do whatever you need to do before the interview to relax—do a vocal warm-up, or do some stretching exercises, or take a short nap or a walk—whatever works best for you.

Take ten or twenty copies of your photos along, with the résumés stapled on the back. If you have photo postcards, business cards, or a videotape of your work, take those along as well. And that calendar you bought to carry everywhere you go—don't forget that. It's unlikely you'll be setting up another appointment while you're in the office, but it won't look good if you need the calendar and don't have it.

Interviews can seem like such important events that actors get charged up or even scared. You want to carry a feeling of calmness into the interview, instead of looking like you're in a hurry or very excited. As you

---

TALKING ABOUT ACTING

I asked one young actor: Do you like to go to auditions?

Ric, age 16: *I hate it and love it all at once. I love the excitement and preparation, and the feeling of elation that comes over me when I do something well during the audition. But I hate it because I know someone is sitting there, analyzing and critiquing my every move, noting every mistake I make.*

If this is true for you, try to focus more on the things you love about acting. Forget about feeling like you're being judged. It's hard to do well when you're super-aware that someone is watching, comparing, and sizing you up. Think of an audition as a very short performance. If you have a way to help yourself feel at ease in front of an audience, use that same method and let yourself "entertain your auditioner." Think of him or her happily sitting in a theater seeing a show you're in. Also, trust in your training and experience, and try to have as much fun at auditions as you do onstage.

sit in the waiting room, take a few deep breaths. Tell yourself that, yes, the interview is important, but it's not the most important thing that will ever happen in your life. If it goes well, and the agent wants to work with you, great! It will probably open a new door in your career. If the agent doesn't seem as interested as you'd like, that's something you can live with. You'll meet many more agents as you go along in your career, and one person's opinion is not all-important.

While you're there, notice what the office is like. Is it clean? Is there a cheerful feeling? You may not want to work with an agent if he or she has a messy office, or if there is a lot of tension in the air. Those qualities can interfere with an agent's ability to run a good business. And how does the agent make you feel? If you enjoy the meeting, you'd probably enjoy working with the agent. But if he or she makes you feel confused or unwelcome in some way, then it might be better to look for a different agent to work with. After all, you want to become a successful actor with a feeling that you're in control of matters like these—not to work with someone who makes you feel powerless or helpless.

Of course, you're friendly, and you answer the agent's questions honestly. You have a short answer prepared for the question they always ask: "So, tell me what you've been doing." Be prepared enough to know what you'd like to talk about. Think about the impression you'd like to make. Try sharing one of your favorite acting experiences.

If you have questions, feel free to ask them. But don't keep thinking up more questions just to keep the interview going. When the agent seems to be wrapping it up, ask if you can keep in touch. Would it be okay to call once a week to see if any auditions have come up? Some agents like actors to call in and check. Others would rather wait and call the actor when they've set up an audition.

If the agent hasn't asked you to leave some photos and résumés, ask if you can leave some. Thank the agent, and as you leave, thank the receptionist or front desk person, too. Why? People change positions often in agencies and casting offices. Next month that front desk person could be working in a television casting office and might remember you.

Now, don't be surprised if you don't hear from the agent right away. A lot of agents like to have a wide range of actors to work with. They don't send you in for an audition until something comes up that they think you are truly right for. Sometimes an actor will interview with an agent, but not hear from the agent for months. But then the actor is perfect for the part that comes up.

Actors can't really expect anything to come of the interview. If something does, and you begin to work with the agent, it will be a bonus. This is one way actors deal with all the times they're turned down in their careers. If you expect very little, you won't feel hurt if very little happens.

A meeting with an agent is mainly an interview, as we've seen. A meeting with a casting director is mainly an audition. Let's turn to that now.

AUDITIONING FOR A CASTING DIRECTOR

There are several different types of casting directors. Some are on the staff of advertising agencies. They generally cast commercials. Some work for television networks and film production companies. And some work on their own on a project-by-project basis. Finding out as much as you can about the person you'll be meeting is a good plan.

You also want to learn what you can about the project you're auditioning for. If it's a new play, a commercial, or a film, find out if you can get the script a day or two ahead of time so that you can prepare. If it's a TV program, watch several episodes beforehand to get an idea of the style of the show and the different types of characters on it. If it's a published play, get a copy of it at the library or a bookstore, and read it several times if you can. The better prepared you are, and the more you know about the project, the more confident you'll feel. And you'll impress the casting person as a professional.

At an audition, the smart actor would dress well and comfortably. You don't want to rush, but take it easy so you'll feel energetic when they call you in. Usually you'll have a few minutes to yourself after you arrive. Someone will likely be auditioning ahead of you. So you'd try to find a private spot where you can warm up a bit and think. If you are auditioning with a monologue or a song, this is when you prepare

TALKING ABOUT ACTING

I asked one young actor: How do you feel about auditions?

Glenn, age 17: *When I audition for someone I know, I'm more relaxed, and I don't feel so pressured. It's easier because they already know what you can do. It's harder with someone I don't know, because I feel like I have to get my foot in the door.*

This is true for most actors. If you pursue acting in community theater or in school, you'll probably audition for people you know. But if you become a professional, particularly in a large city, you'll audition mostly for strangers. You'll need to learn to be as relaxed as you can at auditions. Try some deep breathing, or stretching, or imagining a quiet country setting, until you find a technique that works for you.

so that you can slip quickly into character when your turn comes. (But bear in mind that you want to be yourself when you meet the casting director!)

Cold reading: Reading aloud a scene from the script without rehearsing, to see how you would fit with the role.

If the casting director has you in mind for a particular role, he or she may give you some material to do as a **cold reading.**

You could jump right into it, but it's probably best to ask if you can have a few minutes to look over the material. Then spend that few minutes making some choices about the scene. In this case, your choices should be based on simple ideas. This is not the time to create a whole character you've never explored before, physically and vocally different from anything you've done. You'd ask yourself some simple questions:

• What does the character want?

• How is he or she trying to achieve this goal?

• What is the character really thinking while saying those lines?

Then relax and trust that your talent will come through when you perform the scene.

An audition is simply a performance: It's a two-minute or five-minute scene that you perform for a tiny audience. It isn't the only chance you'll ever get; you'll probably go to hundreds of auditions during the course of your career.

An important idea to remember is that the casting director is most likely on your side. If he or she can present a number of interesting actors to the producer or director, it's a job well done. So don't worry about being judged. Just do your best and have a good time!

THE FOLLOW-UP

After the interview or audition, send a thank-you note. If you can, pick out a detail to mention about the audition—something you really enjoyed, for example. Then begin sending the agent or the casting director those photo postcards of yours. Every three weeks or so is enough to keep in touch. Let people know what you're doing. A lot of casting directors and agents have told actors, "Keep in touch, even if you don't hear from me." You never know when that role will come up that you're perfect for. If you've kept in touch, the agent or casting director will remember you and call you in to audition for it.

Sometimes the casting director is the one who follows up. When he or she thinks that an actor seems right for the role, that actor is given a callback to audition again. If that's the case, you want to wear the same or similar clothing to the callback as you did to the audition. Casting people sometimes find it easier to remember actors by the clothing they wear. In the callback audition, it's best to expand on the work you did at the first audition, rather than change your work altogether. After all, you were called back because they liked the work you did the first time!

Now that you understand what actors go through to get roles, let's see how you'd prepare for a role once you've gotten one.

How
to Prepare
for a Role

WHETHER AN ACTOR HAS BEEN CAST in a play or a film or is simply working on a monologue to use for auditions, he or she must know *how* to work on a role. This is where you need to get some **characterization** basics.

Actors can learn much more about creating the characters they've been hired to play by studying with a teacher or coach. At some point, it will help you as an actor to be in a good training program for a few years. It can be through a college, university, or acting *conservatory* (school), or with a reputable teacher who has his or her own acting *studio* (workshop).

Part of the magic of acting is making it look easy, and this takes a lot of skill, practice, and experience. Of course, good acting is *not* easy, so if you're thinking about moving to a major city to pursue a career, you owe it to yourself to get solid training (see page 63: "Learning Your Craft").

····························
Characterization:
Preparing to act a role by deciding how a character looks, behaves, sounds, thinks, feels—and so on.

GET TO KNOW THE SCRIPT

As a professional actor, the first thing you need to do, whether you've been cast in a role or you're working on an audition piece, is to become familiar with the script. You'll be creating a character and learning your lines later on; for starters, you need to understand the entire story, not just your own character's part in it.

Read the script several times, and get a feeling for the theme—that is, what the author is trying to say. There was a reason the writer wanted to write the play, film, or TV show. Find out what that is. Ask yourself:

- Is the playwright trying to get a message across about the people in the play? About the situation? About the way the world is?

- What are the relationships between the characters like?

- Do any of the characters change, or see things differently, by the end of the piece?

- Are the characters "upper class," down-to-earth, or somewhere in between?

Try to get a feeling for the style of the script as well. Think about questions like these:

- Is it funny, or sad?

- Is it simple, or is there a lot going on throughout?

- Is there a lot of suspense? Does the story build and become more forceful?

- Is the dialogue elegant, or slangy?

The more information you can get about the story before you start on your own characterization, the better your character will fit in with the whole piece.

STARTING ON YOUR ROLE

One of the most important approaches to doing a role is to find a way you can "connect" to the character. There ought to be something within you that is touched by *who* the character is, or what the character wants or believes. You need to be able to understand why a character does what he or she does. Does this person do good works that benefit others? Or commit crimes to get what he or she wants? You base your answers to these questions on your reading of the script.

One of the things actors love about their jobs is the unusual experience of "getting inside other people's heads." They discover sides of themselves they never knew existed, and then use them to create a unique character. Through acting, you can portray a murderer or a saint, a president or a poor person—without any of the realities you'd have if you were actually that person!

Again, to begin getting in touch with the character, ask yourself questions. As you gain more experience with characterization, you'll know quickly what kinds of questions will be most helpful to you. Here are some that most actors would start with:

- What's the most important thing that the character does in the play?

- Why does the character do what he does?

- What does she want most, and what lengths will she go to to get it?

- What are the character's relationships like? Close to other people or distant from them?

- Does he have any strong beliefs about himself? About the world? About other people?

- Does she get what she wants by the end of the play? What is her feeling about that?

- How do your character's actions and behavior connect with the author's theme or message?

Motivation: The reason a character performs the actions he or she does in the script. (See "Blocking," pages 47-49.)

The more thinking you can do about your character and his or her behavior and **motivation,** the more interesting your portrayal will be.

THE PHYSICAL CHARACTER

As actors gain experience, they learn different ways of expressing characters physically. Some characters move quickly, with a bouncy rhythm or nervous energy. Others move more slowly—some with care, some because they are afraid. If you sit in a mall for any length of time to watch people go by, you'll begin to notice that some walk swiftly, others with weariness. Some move smoothly and some jerkily.

Along with rhythm, you can study posture: Does your character stand tall and move gracefully? Or does he or she stoop, or lean to one side? There are many possibilities for choices you can make about how your character moves and gestures:

- Is the character proud of who he is and what he does? (If he is, he would probably stand up straight and move with energy.)

- Or does he try to be noticed as little as possible? (This kind of behavior might result from fear. Or it might be a dishonest person's way of hiding something he did behind someone's back. Such a character might even sneak around.)

- Is the character generally in a hurry, trying to get too much done in a little time? Or is she relaxed, taking things as they come?

- Where would the character's worries show up in his or her body?

An actor must be careful not to make the physical choices too big or too obvious. You can end up looking more like a cartoon than a person. Some of the best physical work done by great **character actors** is so carefully performed that you hardly notice the details, which are often called *nuances*. They are subtle, but they still have an effect.

Character actor: An actor who is known for creating unusual and interesting characters. What great character actors in today's films spring to mind for you?

As you sharpen your own skill at observing people, you'll develop a sort of mental CD-ROM you can refer to for character "data." You'll also want to learn to listen to people's voices. An unusual voice can be the perfect finishing touch for a character. Here are some questions that can help you form an image of how the character behaves vocally:

- Does he speak as quickly as possible? Is she afraid others will interrupt?

- Or does the character form thoughts and words slowly, speaking in a deliberate way?

- What area of the country is the character from? People from the South speak differently from other areas of the country. Characters have regional *accents* and *dialects*. And you can hear differences in the speed and pitch (highness or lowness of voice) with which they speak.

- Are the character's lips tight, as if he or she doesn't want to let the words out?

- Does he or she generally speak softly or loudly? (If softly, make sure the audience can still hear you!)

THE CHARACTER'S THINKING

As you can see, there are many details involved in building a character. An actor also needs to explore different ideas about how a character thinks:

- Does he or she have a quick mind?

- Does he or she make decisions only after much thought, or suddenly?

- Is the character very intelligent, just average, or below average?

- Can the character see things through "other people's eyes," or only from his or her point of view?

- Does the character think clearly and correctly about the story's events? Is he or she confused, mistaken, or completely fooled?

There are many, many choices you can make about a character. As you make them, you *build* the character.

Some of the character's qualities will be fairly obvious after you've read the script a few times. Other qualities may take more digging. Some will be pointed out by the director when you are rehearsing. You'll discover new choices when you are working with the rest of the cast. And there will even be other ideas you come up with to fill in the details that aren't suggested in the script.

The point is to explore. As a skilled professional actor, you'd explore as many possibilities as you could.

Near the end of the rehearsal period, you'll pretty much want to stick to the best choices you've discovered. Once you're working in front of an audience or a camera, you'll be more comfortable if you have a fairly set structure that you've given yourself. The ideas you've decided on for your character will make up much of your performance.

Now we'll find out what it's like to be in rehearsal.

In
Rehearsal

THE PROCESS OF REHEARSING can be one of the most creative experiences you'll ever have. In the theater, you'll usually rehearse a play or musical for four to six weeks. The exception is in summer stock, where you may rehearse for only a week or two. In film, the rehearsal plan is usually set up by the director, and may last from a few days up to several weeks.

LEARNING LINES

Different actors approach rehearsing in different ways. Some actors like to learn all their lines, if they can, before rehearsals begin. Other actors prefer to learn the lines as they learn the **blocking.**

Blocking: Movement patterns given to the actors by the director to set up a specific "picture" that helps the audience understand the scene.

There is a good and a not so good side to both methods. If you learn the lines first, you've completed a very important part of the process. You're free to use your rehearsal time in creating your character. But if you're not careful, you may learn the lines in a too-specific way. You may become too set in the speech rhythms and tones you've chosen. Then it can become hard to allow yourself to change as your character develops.

If you wait to learn the lines during rehearsals, you'll be learning your lines and blocking together, and creating your character and working off the other actors, all at the same time. This can make it easier to put together many of the elements of your performance. If you choose this method, it's still a good idea to become as familiar with the script as you can before rehearsals begin. That way, you have a basic understanding of the story and the characters.

As you act more roles, you'll begin to learn how you work best. Each actor works in a different way, and once you find a way that works well for you, go with it. The work of performing and going to auditions and interviews can jangle anyone's nerves a bit, so actors are better off if they can find a reliable way of learning lines and creating a character.

BLOCKING

Blocking is the pattern of movement the director gives the actors in rehearsals. It can include crossing to another part of the stage, entering or exiting, and sitting down or standing up. The director may give you instructions such as "cross downstage right," or "sit in the up center chair."

Here is a diagram of the standard stage directions in the theater:

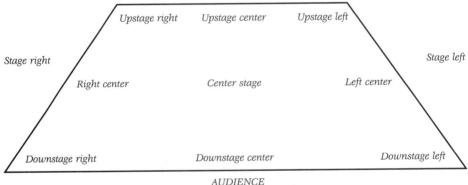

You'll notice that the directions of left and right are reversed from the viewpoint of the audience. When you're standing onstage facing the audience, "stage right" will refer to your right, "stage left" to your left.

One important part of an actor's job is to find a motivation, or a purpose, for each piece of blocking the director assigns. That is, there is a reason for the character to make that particular move.

For instance, if the director has given you blocking to stand up when another character enters the room, you need to choose a good reason for your character to stand up at that time. Otherwise, you'll just look like you're standing up because the director told you to. Perhaps your char-

Photo by Stan Sherer

The blocking in this scene is very unusual, but each actor has found a motivation to make his or her position make sense.

acter loves or hates the other one, and is excited or dismayed to see that person. Or perhaps your character thinks of himself as a gentleman, and rises whenever a woman enters. Or perhaps your character sees it's raining when the door opens, and suddenly remembers she left the top down on her convertible.

Choosing motivations is one of the most creative and fun aspects of the actor's work. Trying different choices in rehearsal, to find out what works best for the character and the scene, you can experiment with simple and obvious motivations, and you can play with very complex or unusual ones. Actors trust their own feelings to tell them when they've found something that works. With a good motivation, it "seems right" that the character stands or moves at that particular point in the story.

THE ACTOR'S CREATIVITY

The lines you speak and the director's blocking form the "skeleton" of the play, film, or show you're in. They're the elements which generally remain the same through the rehearsals and the performances. Unless you're working with the author of the script, or unless the director is very flexible, you should perform the lines and blocking without making changes.

What you can play with creatively as an actor are your use of your voice, your rhythms (faster or slower, with or without pauses), gestures, posture, or "body language"—anything that is not a part of the skeleton. Most actors like to play a lot with choices in the early rehearsals. They try a lot of different ways of doing things, and then begin to "firm up" their choices as the rehearsals get close to the performance of the piece for the audience or the camera.

When a play is in performance, it runs much more smoothly if each actor knows pretty well what the other actors are going to do. Mistakes and odd moments will happen, but the more the rhythm of the show is "set," the easier it is for actors to deal with things they weren't expecting.

FEEDBACK FROM THE DIRECTOR

Directors will jot down notes during rehearsals and then read them back to the actors afterward. This is called *giving notes* to the actors. Basically, notes are the changes the director wants the actors to work on in the next rehearsal. These might include blocking changes, new ideas to try, lines that were spoken incorrectly, and character suggestions.

When the director gives you a note, you can ask questions if you need him or her to make something clearer. Then think about the notes and begin working on them as a sort of homework. The best actors always try to bring the change into their work in their next rehearsal.

Sometimes actors do not agree with the director. During notes is not the time to dispute with him or her. If you have a problem with one of the notes you're given, you must find a time to discuss it with the director in private. Just say "Okay," or "Thank you," and remind yourself to speak with the director later.

Sometimes a director has a fixed idea of how a scene should go, and won't give that up even if there is a better way. If you were in this situa-

TALKING ABOUT ACTING

I asked a young actor: Is there anything you don't like about acting?

Iona, age 12: *I hate having an image of how I want to play a scene in my head, and the director is dead set on doing it a different way that I don't think works as well.*

This can definitely be a problem, even on a professional level. Often, the director is trying to achieve a vision of the script that you can't see from your view as one actor in the show. It's hard to look at your own work from the outside. What you feel is coming across may not be what others see. Part of the director's job is to be another set of eyes, and the actor's job is to make good use of the feedback from the director.

tion, you'd need to find a time that you could talk with the director alone. The actor should never appear to be "showing up" the director, or making him or her feel put down in front of the whole cast. Ask if you can try the scene your way. Most directors will let you at least try, and some may see what you're trying to do.

You might ask some of the other actors if they agree. They'll tell you whether or not you're the only one who feels as you do. But remember that the director does have the authority to make the final choices about scenes. You can explore to some degree, but if you change what the director told you to do on opening night or during filming, he or she probably won't want to work with you again.

The director's job is to bring about the best possible performance. Sometimes the reason you get a particular note may not become clear for a while. It takes the cast's efforts some time to blend together into the finished performance, and the director has a view of the entire piece that no one actor can have. Sometimes you just have to trust that the director is doing a good job.

REHEARSAL ROUGH SPOTS

Not all directors are equally good. Sometimes major problems develop in rehearsals, and actors have to talk to someone whose advice they trust— a close friend, their agent, or a union official.

Directors are usually seen as powerful people, and sometimes they are. But in the real world of show business they are not supposed to scream at actors, mistreat them, or put them down. If this happened to you in the rehearsal of a play, you could get advice on how to deal with it from the actors' union, Actors' Equity Association. In most union productions, the cast elects one actor who will represent them and act as a link to the union. You could take your problem to this person. You could have talks with people at the union office if the problem became very serious.

In rare cases, the union cannot solve a problem. Then, if you decided you could no longer work with the director, you could quit the show.

Problems are rarely so bad there is no way to work things out. But even among professionals, in the theater, in film, and in TV, things do not always go smoothly. Actors have unions they can turn to, and other people, too, when they need some help. You can read more about unions on pages 111 to 114.

I asked: Is there anything you don't like about acting?

Howard, age 15: *The only thing I don't like about being in some shows is that some people in the cast don't seem to want to be involved in it. It's very frustrating—no matter what kind of part you have—to show up at a rehearsal for a play that's opening in a week, and half the cast don't know their lines very well, and the other half don't even bother showing up.*

Good point! It sounds like the actors who don't show up don't really want to be actors. Or else they don't have much respect for the others in the cast. If you don't show up, you are wasting other people's time. If you were in a professional show, your behavior would probably get you fired. You do hear of some big stars who don't show others the respect they expect to receive from them. But it's unlikely that people truly do respect them.

If you have a role in a non-union production and run into a problem, talk to an acting teacher or someone else you trust for advice.

TECH REHEARSALS AND DRESS REHEARSALS

In the theater, technical rehearsals take place in the last few days before opening night. They're often called *tech* rehearsals for short. Their purpose is to combine the technical elements of the production, such as the lighting, sound, scenery, and costumes, with the play for the first time. Everything can be examined for how it adds to the whole. Equipment can be tested. Mistakes can be seen clearly, and the solutions to them can be discussed.

In early tech rehearsals, actors may be asked to stand in certain positions onstage while technicians adjust the lights. Another rehearsal may be spent getting used to the costumes and props. If you are rehearsing a script set in an earlier period in history, wearing clothing that will be similar to your costume in rehearsals can help you get a better feel for your character.

If all goes well, the *dress rehearsal* will occur a night or two before opening night, and everyone will get a chance to feel what the real performance will be like. Keep in mind as you work with the tech people that their contribution to the show is very important. Without costumes or light or props, the play would not be complete. The work that they do helps you do your best work as an actor.

In film and TV, the tech people include the camera operators, the makeup artists, the sound technicians, and so on. Actors owe these skilled people as much respect and courtesy as they would give the director and other actors.

Tech week can be very strenuous and nerve-wracking. Actors need to take especially good care of their health as opening night comes closer. Everyone is excited during tech week. As the play goes through the last

few rehearsals, everyone is gearing up for the magical time when the play comes alive in front of an audience for the first time.

If you are cast in a "period" play, you'll probably rehearse in clothing that's similar to what your costume will be like (a long dress, a judge's robe, and so on).

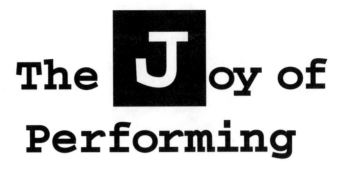

The Joy of Performing

IMAGINE MAKING YOUR LIVING AS AN ACTOR. You may be working in film and television and on the stage. The film and television jobs would pay you rather well, and you'd make good money doing a commercial now and then. But now you're working in the theater. The theater pays less well, but it offers something special: performing in front of a live audience.

You've worked on a new play for several weeks—learning your lines and blocking, working with props and costumes, and finally rehearsing under the lights. It's time to go out on the stage where many great actors have appeared before you, and show what you can do!

BEFORE THE SHOW

Everyone is usually a little nervous on opening night. Dealing with costumes and props and remembering cues still take concentration. No one can predict how the audience will respond. This is a time when you as an actor must trust yourself. You have to feel that you've learned your lines and worked hard enough to know that the play will go fine.

If there are things you're unsure of in the few days before the play opens, it's best to let the director know. Sometimes actors do need some extra rehearsal time to work out a scene. You don't want to simply hope that, somehow, it'll come out right.

The director or stage manager gives you a *call* time to get to the theater for this opening night performance, and every other performance as well. Unless there's a group warm-up, you need to find time while you're getting ready to warm up your voice and body. Some actors like to do a warm-up when they arrive, and then get into character while putting on their makeup and costume. Others put their makeup and costume on first, then warm up as close as possible to **curtain time.**

Curtain time: The time the show begins. This term is used whether there's a curtain or not.

The stage manager gives you "warnings" before curtain time. These usually come a half hour, fifteen minutes, and five minutes before the show begins. That way you can pace yourself in getting ready. Next, the stage manager will *ask for places* at two minutes before curtain time. This simply means that he or she requests that you go to the place backstage from which you'll be entering. If you don't enter until later in the show, you may be able to wait in the dressing room or green room until a few moments before you enter.

With the help of the large mirrors in their backstage dressing room, these actors are putting on makeup before a performance.

OPENING NIGHT ENERGY

Now comes the moment you've worked toward. You take a deep breath, relax, and let your energy and enjoyment flow. The more enjoyment you have onstage, the more the audience will enjoy your performance. (If the play is a tragedy you may not enjoy it in the same way, but you'll get caught up in the action.)

Opening night nerves are very natural, because of the excitement. Forgetting a line or missing a moment may be a mistake, but it's not a disgrace. It's simply part of the process of putting on a play. One of the major reasons that audiences go to plays is to be entertained by live actors onstage, where anything can happen. So even though you may be very focused and working hard, you can make a goof. The best thing to do if someone makes a mistake is just to forget about it and go on with the play. The audience is there to see your live performance, not a perfectly timed, perfectly edited, perfectly set film performance.

You may have long stretches of time between the scenes in which you appear onstage. You have to remember to keep your focus on the play even if you do other activities. Some actors read or play cards between their scenes. There are stories of actors who got so caught up in a card game that they missed an entrance. The people who were onstage waiting for them had to **ad lib.**

An ad lib can be anything from what the weather is like to gossip about the character who will be coming onstage. This creates a good reason to stop the instant the character enters, and to continue with the action of the play. Some actors are better at ad-libbing than others. If you aren't, don't worry. The main thing if you do have to ad lib is to carry on within the world of the play.

Ad lib: A line or lines that actors make up on the spot. When an actor forgets a line, or is supposed to make an entrance and doesn't, the other actors can lose their place or have no way to continue the action if they do not invent dialogue or action. This is called ad-libbing.

There are actors who become known for being late often or for missing their entrances. This is not a good reputation to have. Your career could suffer, because you might find it difficult to get cast. Do your job with a professional attitude.

And have a good time too! After that first performance comes the party that everyone's been waiting for: the opening night party. Now that you're past the jitters of opening the show, it will be even more fun!

TALKING ABOUT ACTING

I asked an actor in high school: What part of acting is hardest for you?

Jeremy, age 17: *The hardest part is how much of yourself you really have to use. Before I'd done it, I assumed you were reciting lines. But having done it now, it's a lot different. When I come home from having done an emotional scene, I don't want to do homework, wash dishes, or make my bed. I just want to sleep!*

Acting can take a lot out of you. And that's on top of the auditioning, which takes a lot of energy. And you have to make a living doing other jobs until you're earning money as an actor. If you're trying to figure out if a career is a good move for you, think about the fun of rehearsals and the joy of performing. It keeps a lot of actors going. Will it be enough for you?

THE RUN OF THE PLAY

As you "run" the play over a period of nights, weeks, or months, you and the other actors will get more and more comfortable with the lines, the blocking, and each other. You'll probably find that you are deepening your character, just by being in the role night after night. Also, you will gain some freedom to play a little bit with things like your *timing:* You might:

- Make a move more quickly or slowly.

- Say a line faster or more slowly.

- Experiment with the length of a pause before an important line.

If you're in a comedy, even a millisecond change in the timing of a line can make a big difference between whether the audience just twitters or howls with laughter. (Of course, the action that leads up to the line is important, too.) Working with timing in comedies and all kinds of plays is one of the most enjoyable aspects of acting.

One change that actors are *not* permitted to make is to rewrite any of the lines in the play. And we've already seen that the blocking must stay the way the director wanted it. Making changes in these areas can start to throw the entire play out of whack.

Good actors always find that there's plenty of room to be creative with their character's behavior and thoughts. If you get a role in a show that runs for a year or more, you may end up fighting boredom more than the jitters. But remember: You can always go into more detail about what the character is thinking, what he or she believes, what he's trying to get, what she's really "all about." You should not let the show become a drag for you. This is not a problem in acting in a film or TV show (unless a series you do runs for many seasons). But in the theater, each person who bought a ticket should see the freshest performance you can give.

Next let's take a look at some of the bumps in the road of show business and how actors starting out keep themselves on balance.

Keeping
Your Balance

ACTING IS A BUSINESS that has a lot to do with *personality,* so people in show business tend to put up with unusual personalities more than people in other fields, like banking and medicine, would. Because of this, show business attracts people who may be hard to work with or difficult to trust. Sometimes these people may hold positions of power—they may be directors or producers, casting directors or agents, or even teachers.

Let's say you're starting out as a young actor. It's good to know ahead of time that you may run into some people you don't like, or situations that upset you. This section is not intended to scare you away, but to show you why you need to be careful in dealing with people in your acting career. How do you keep your balance in this business?

TRUST YOUR FEELINGS

If you have a sense that something's fishy about a situation, your sense is probably correct. Your feelings can at least alert you that there might be a problem. Let's look at some possible harmful situations that could come up. Suppose someone wants you to audition in a private home. Sounds odd, and unsafe, doesn't it? Especially for women, if you live in a large city, it's best to be careful about where you go. In New York City or Los Angeles, there are some neighborhoods you'd probably never visit, for any reason. If you decide to move to a large city, ask a friend who's lived there a while which areas you should avoid.

Sometimes actors want to work so badly that they'll do almost anything. Then they often get hurt in the end. Just remember: You don't want to be one of those actors who will risk their well-being in order to succeed.

Any time people push you to do something you don't feel right about, such as auditioning at their residence, or taking any of your clothes off, trust your *instincts*—one of the reasons you have them is to keep you safe. You don't ever have to do something that someone asks you to do, if it doesn't feel right.

You may be asked to audition at night. Unless you know that the company often auditions at night—there are some that do—you need to find out more. The theater newspapers do their best to keep from printing any ads or casting notices that are not on the level, but sometimes one can slip through. Trust your instincts and ask other actors what they think.

WHEN THEY ASK FOR MONEY

There are people who cheat actors. Their tricks, or *scams,* aren't dangerous, but you can lose money. Watch out for anyone who offers you a shortcut to getting something that normally takes you some time when you follow the rules. One example is a union card. People have offered actors union membership cards, which actors usually earn by working. They say they know ways to get around the rules, then they take the actor's $600 or $1,000 and disappear.

You wouldn't want to believe any agent who says he or she will make you a star if you pay a certain amount of money up front. Some of these agents will tell you they'll put together a book of actors' photos that important producers will see, and this is what the money is for. Some honest agencies do create actor-photo books, but anyone who promises to make you a star is only looking for your money.

Agents do business in connection with the actors' unions and have to follow the union rules. So the best way to find out if an agent has a good reputation is to call one of the unions. Actors' *managers* are different; they are *not* bound by any rules, so you'll need to be a little more alert when dealing with them.

Actors just starting out often like the idea of hooking up with a theater company. (These companies are usually small and may be called *acting troupes* or *ensembles* or some other name.) But some companies will offer you membership if you pay a certain amount of dues. This practice is another fishy deal. There is no danger involved, but some professionals would tell you it's a mistake to pay people so that you can work for them.

Some of these small theater companies do fair work, but so do many where actors work for free. And many companies do pay actors something, even if it's just subway or bus fare.

If you are new to a city, becoming a member of a theater company can be a way to get to know other actors and get some experience. Just find out about a company before you join. If it has a bad reputation, stay away. Most of the casting directors and agents in the city will probably know that actors must pay to join and just won't bother to come see those performances.

Most people who work in the acting business are good people like yourself. You may never be in a harmful situation, but it's always best to be alert and be prepared if trouble turns up.

HOW TO STAY SANE

Most of the people you meet as an actor will earn your trust. But some of them will make you wonder if you're losing your mind. As you know by now, show business does attract people who enjoy "playing games" with others. Some are on "power trips" and may mistreat you. Some directors, producers, and even acting teachers know that many actors will do almost anything to get a job. They feel powerful if they're in a position to offer the actor something, or to turn the actor down.

You can often spot these people long before they do you any harm. But some actors have a problem spotting them at first. Let's try to understand what happens.

Some ways of being treated badly may be familiar to you. There is a lot of tension in some families. Parents may yell or say they're going to hurt someone. Even worse behavior can be considered normal in some families.

If this is true in your family, you may think it's acceptable behavior. It is not. You don't ever have to allow anyone to hit you. If anyone in your family, or anyone else, is yelling at you or calling you names, you have the right to walk away. There are always better ways to settle things or to express anger.

Some actors have been screamed at in an acting class. Or they have worked with an agent or another person in the business who yells or threatens them. If this happens to you, remember: It is not because of any fault of your own. It's not because you've made a mistake. It's because that person enjoys putting other people down.

The next thing you need to do is to get away from that person. And stay away. There are always more people to meet in the business, and the more you move away from those who are "bad news," the more you'll find people you'll really enjoy working with.

A teacher or an agent may threaten you with the idea that if you don't do what he or she wants, you'll never get another job as an actor. This is simply a game that person plays to feel like a big shot. If people like that can get you to believe what they're saying, then you're at their mercy and they feel stronger.

Usually, the reputation of someone like that is pretty well known to other people in the business. And that means the person has little or no real power with others.

It can be hard to spot a phony. If you were starting out and landed in a situation like this, it could just be confusing to you. In that case, you'd need to find someone to talk to right away. You could talk to a close friend who is also an actor. Or contact a teacher or college professor that you felt comfortable with. Talk about the behavior of the person who is confusing you or giving you a hard time. Ask for advice. Some people don't like talking about these kinds of issues. Keep trying until you find someone who will help you.

You could also call one of the actors' unions, or a theater newspaper such as *Back Stage*. You would ask them to refer you to someone. The Actors' Fund is another organization that helps actors.

Just don't let a situation go on until you feel like you can't get out of it without getting hurt. Actors can often feel that everyone else is in charge of what happens to them. But if you ever

TALKING ABOUT ACTING

I asked one young actor I met: What do you like about acting?

Lindsay, age 13: *The best thing about acting, for me, is being able to sort of "escape," so I can be someone besides myself for a change.*

This is something a lot of actors say they love about their work. They can try on different personalities as they do new roles. Acting is a wonderful way to learn about yourself. Still, it's important not to think acting is the *only* way you can express yourself. Some actors start to feel they're not worth anything if they're not acting. You don't want to rely on acting to make you feel good.

land in a situation where you are being mistreated, you must not be afraid to say, "I have to leave now." You can be in charge and walk out. People you don't want to work with can't hold you back from getting other jobs someplace else.

A career in acting can be very rewarding, but not if you have to work with negative people. Do your best to stay focused on the healthy and the positive. You'll stay sane and have a better chance of success.

Learning
Your Craft

WE'VE ALREADY SAID THAT AN ACTOR NEEDS TRAINING. The truth is, many actors continue to work on their craft even when they've begun to make a living. Let's discuss the first training you can get as an actor, then look at the ways you can continue with your training.

TRAINING IN HIGH SCHOOL

If you're serious about having a career as an actor, you may be able to go to a performing arts high school. You can begin your training as quickly as possible. Competition at performing arts high schools can be strong, and you'll need to keep up your grades just as you would at any other high school.

Many regular high schools also have good theater classes or clubs. Even if you're not in high school yet, check to see if your local high school has a drama club. This is a good way to get started acting and meet others who like theater.

High school theater classes can give you some good first lessons in acting. But you'll also want to get some training that goes deeper. You can check the Yellow Pages to see if there are any after-school theater classes or programs for young people in your area.

Or you might do some work or act a role at a nearby theater. It might be a professional theater, but it will probably be a community theater. Many of the adults who do community theater have been acting and directing for years, and you can learn a lot watching and acting with them. You'll want to see as many shows as you can, too. Sitting in the

I asked a young actor who has a career: Are there any comments you'd give to young actors?

Linda, age 24:*Go to college! That way, if the whole show-biz thing doesn't work out, you have a degree of some sort to fall back on.*

If you're not able to attend a performing arts school, it's still a very good idea to go to college, wherever you can. Going to college (or a community college) will give you a broader understanding of the world. The more you know about different subjects and ideas, the better your acting will be. Getting a college degree can also be very helpful in getting a job that supports you while you look for acting work.

audience, you can learn what makes you believe an actor's performance. And you'll begin to figure out what doesn't work, as well.

If you're already in high school, ask one of your teachers about the Arts Recognition and Talent Search. This program is run by the National Foundation for Advancement in the Arts, located in Miami, Florida. They award scholarships to high school seniors in theater, musical theater, dance, music, the visual arts, and writing. The students who get the awards may get a chance to go to a major acting school, such as the Juilliard School or New York University, in New York City.

If your teacher doesn't have any information about the program, you can write to them:

National Foundation for Advancement in the Arts
800 Brickell Ave., Suite 500
Miami, Florida 33131

And, of course, you want to start to thinking ahead: Should you study acting in college or in an acting program at a special school, such as a performing-arts institute?

TRAINING IN COLLEGE

Your best bet for college, if you're planning to be a professional actor, is one of the schools that are part of the National League of Professional Training Programs.

These schools have set up their programs to give the best training possible to actors who will be pursuing a career. Here is a list of some of them:

American Conservatory Theatre, in San Francisco, California

Boston University, in Boston, Massachusetts

Carnegie-Mellon University, in Pittsburgh, Pennsylvania

The Juilliard School, in New York City

New York University Tisch School of the Arts, in New York City

This director is working closely with actors in a rehearsal. If you were to go to a school that is connected with a professional theater, you'd probably get to work with professional directors..

North Carolina School of the Arts, in Winston-Salem, North Carolina

Southern Methodist University, in Dallas, Texas

State University of New York, in Purchase, New York

Temple University in Philadelphia, Pennsylvania

University of California, San Diego, in La Jolla, California

University of Washington School of Drama, in Seattle, Washington

Yale School of Drama, in New Haven, Connecticut

Each school publishes its own catalogue, but you can get a brochure describing each of these programs from:

The League of Professional Theatre Training Programs
1860 Broadway
Suite 1515
New York, NY 10023

These schools train actors to become professionals and then give them a chance to audition for agents and casting directors near the end of the program. If you can go to one of these schools, you'll have a much better chance of getting your career off the ground in the beginning. Most agents and casting directors have a high regard for graduates of these schools. This doesn't mean that if you go to a different college, you don't have a chance at building a good career. But these schools can get you started a little bit faster.

Another plan is to go to a training program that is not part of a regular college. These kinds of programs are also geared to actors who will pursue a career. Some are members of the National Association of Schools of Theatre. These schools offer two- or three-year programs. Each is located in a large city, so you'll learn all about living in one, before you even begin your career.

Here is a list of some of these schools—you can write to them to find out what they require to get in:

National Shakespeare Conservatory
440 Lafayette Street
New York, NY 10003

Neighborhood Playhouse School of Theatre
340 E. 54th Street
New York, NY 10022

New Actors Workshop
259 W. 30th Street
New York, NY 10001

Circle in the Square Theatre School
1633 Broadway
New York, NY 10019-6795

National Conservatory of Dramatic Arts
1556 Wisconsin Ave. NW
Washington, DC 20007

American Conservatory Theatre
30 Grant Ave., 6th Floor
San Francisco, CA 94102

National Theatre Conservatory
1050 13th Street
Denver, CO 80204

Eugene O'Neill Theater Center
305 Great Neck Road
Waterford, CT 06385

Boston Conservatory
8 The Fenway
Boston, MA 02215

ANOTHER NETWORK OF SCHOOLS

There is another network of theater schools, the University/Resident Theatre Association. These schools offer actors the chance to work with professional companies during their training. Most offer undergraduate degrees. One of the nicest things about them is that you'll have an opportunity to audition for a group of masters degree programs and resident theater companies all at one time. People from the schools and the companies gather once a year in New York, Los Angeles, and Chicago to see the actors audition. This saves having to travel all over the country auditioning—you can audition for a number of groups at once.

There are thirty-one schools and companies that belong to the University/Resident Theatre Association. You can find out more by writing to:

University/Resident Theatre Association
1560 Broadway, Suite 903
New York, NY 10036
(212) 221-1130
E-mail: URTA@aol.com

Get as much information as you can about any training program you're thinking about. Your early training will form the basis for the acting technique you use throughout your career.

ACTING CLASSES

Whether you're taking classes to polish up your skills as an actor, or taking classes for fun, there are many kinds of teachers and classes to choose from. In most classes, you'll work on acting by doing scenes, whether they are from plays, films, or commercial scripts.

Acting classes aren't all the same. There are classes in improvisation, acting technique, and **scene study**. There are also classes in different *period* styles—that is, historical periods. For example, Shakespeare's plays are period plays, and to do them well you need to learn how people moved and behaved many centuries ago. And there are film and commercial technique classes that teach you special skills for performing before a camera.

Scene study: In this type of acting class, the teacher asks you to pick a scene from a play, or assigns you a scene, and helps you and a partner work on it. Then, any work you do on your acting technique is done when it's needed in that scene.

Every teacher has his or her own style or method. When you're beginning to learn acting, it's a good idea to take classes with several teachers. This way you can get a feel for the ways that different teachers approach acting. Then you can decide to study with one of them. Finding a teacher that you work with well is like finding a good friend: It takes some time to get to know that teacher. Usually, you'll feel more comfortable with some than with others.

Most acting classes run for several weeks or several months. Teachers of technique will teach you some steps to take in developing a character.

Photo by Jim Gipe

An actor needs to start training before beginning a career. Even if you have gotten training, look into a class that meets one or two nights a week. As time goes by, it's a good idea to go on taking classes—maybe in a different area, such as movement or dance.

Often, you'll learn about your **sense memory** and how to strengthen it. In the first meetings of an acting class, the teacher will often take you through some exercises, and then will begin to teach you acting technique. The teacher might suggest a specific monologue for you to work on and bring to class, or you might be asked to work on a scene with a partner outside class, then perform it in class so that the teacher (and sometimes the other students) can comment and make suggestions. Usually you and your partner will begin by performing the entire scene for the class. Then the teacher may work with you on specific parts of the scene, or *beats*. Or he or she may help you work on your character or relationship in some other way.

Many good actors think of acting classes as a place to take risks, to play, to try different ways of doing things. It's better to try an approach and have it work poorly in the class than on a job that you've been hired for. If you watch the work of the other actors in

Sense memory: When you recall an experience you've stored in your memory and use it in your acting, you are using your sense memory. For example, in some scenes you may need to act being cold. Your senses have been affected by cold in the past, so you begin reacting the same way—by shivering or rubbing your hands. Actors' performances are more realistic when their past sensations become tools in this way.

the class, you can learn a lot about what works in a scene, and what does not. Pay attention to the other actors and you might notice someone you'd really like to work with because of his or her talent, skill, or style. You can ask the teacher to assign a scene for you to work on together.

As you get more training and experience as an actor, you'll find out which techniques work well for you, and which do not. If an actor tried to use every acting technique, his or her performances would be nothing but a hodge-podge. So use what works for you and forget the rest. Actors need to develop their own style as they go along, and learn to trust their inner sense of what is right.

Taking an acting or scene study class is a good way to learn the self-discipline a professional actor must have. If you're working on a scene with a partner outside class, take care not to goof around and neglect your work. Remember, the actors you see on the stage and screen do a lot of outside work on their roles. You'll get much more out of your acting classes if you work hard even when you're not there, learning the craft of acting on your own.

And if you'll be going into acting as a career, the better your acting is, the better your chances of being hired will be.

Money and Work

MONEY CAN BE DIFFICULT for actors to think about. Maybe you've heard a lot about how hard it is for actors to make a living. It is true that most professional actors cannot get by on acting jobs alone. Most of them must find other jobs to make enough to live on, in order to do what they love: acting. You need to look at this business with realism: As an actor, you too will probably be doing other jobs to make money. At the same time, you'll pursue your career.

IDEAS ABOUT MONEY

Let's start out with two ideas that will help you think about the money side of your acting career. The first idea is: If you believe in your heart that you *can* make a living at acting, you will have the right attitude for success.

The second idea is: If you believe in your heart that you'll *never* make a living at acting, you never will. Why? Because that's how you'll make your efforts turn out.

It's not easy to see reality clearly and still not fall into the trap of expecting to be poor just because you're an actor. It's important not to stick yourself with a *not* belief: that you're *not* going to have any money. *Not* beliefs of this kind that get set in your mind can be found in every area of your life, if you look for them:

- "I don't have any fun."

- "I can never find a nice boyfriend (or girlfriend)."

- "My hair always looks messy."

If there's something you don't like about your life, say to yourself: "That's a problem"—and then look for ways to improve it. Don't just assume your hair is going to be messy for the rest of your life! There are many steps you can take to fix almost any problem.

When it comes to money and work, you need *can* beliefs. The trick is to allow yourself to have as much money as you want and need, even though you're an actor. It *can* be done, if you look ahead.

MAKING A LIVING

We always hear about actors who hit it big and make enormous amounts of money. None of them could have started out being sure they'd get rich. It's smart to assume you will not make your living right away as an actor.

So, what other things do you like to do that might support you while you build your career? Remember that becoming an actor will take a certain amount of money for classes and photos. And it will take a lot of time to go to interviews and auditions and work on monologues and roles. So you'll want some kind of job that pays you well and allows you some free time for auditions.

Temporary agency:
A "temp" business has a number of client companies and hires you for only a day, a week, or a month to work at one of those companies.

Many actors support themselves as waiters. If you get hired at a top-quality restaurant, the tips can be enough along with the salary to give you the money you need. Other actors work as secretaries, word processors, and proofreaders in jobs they got from a **temporary agency.**

"Temp" jobs can be an excellent way to support your acting career. They give you flexibility. In large cities they may pay pretty well if you have good skills. And it's usually easy to get work with temp agencies, even if you've had to take some time off for acting work. Look in the Yellow Pages under "Employment Agencies—Temporary" to see if there are any in your area.

If you're thinking of moving to one of the major cities, make it a point soon after you move to visit the agencies and apply for work. You can register with a number of different ones. This will bring you more chances to work when you want to, and you won't be tied down to one agency.

A lot of actors like the variety they get from working at temp agencies. You may work at a bank one week, a law firm the next, and so on. If you can learn typing, computer, or proofreading skills before you move to a big city, do it. If you can learn how waiters serve people at fine restaurants, you may find work without a lot of trouble.

Some actors create their own businesses. They give massages, deliver singing telegrams, take care of people's pets, and so on, as they pursue their careers. This can be a great approach, because if you have your own business, you can work when it fits into your day. The only thing to watch out for is spending all your time and energy building up that business. You can lose sight of what you wanted to do with your acting career.

As you can see, it will help you to know what you'd like to do to support yourself before you begin a career.

THE NUMBERS

As a young person, you might not have much experience with money yet. Parents don't often share a lot of news about the bills they're paying. How much money will you need to pay the bills each month if you live in New York or Los Angeles? Here is a list of basic expenses:

Rent	$800 and up (may be cheaper if you share with others)
Groceries	$100 and up (doesn't include eating out)
Gas and electric bills	$60 and up
Transportation	$75 and up (subways in New York; car in Los Angeles)
Telephone	$40 and up
Answering service	$20
Personal care	$15 (soap, shampoo, toothpaste, etc.)

The total for one month is $1,110! And these are just the very basics you need in order to live—it leaves out costs for:

- Home furnishings

- Entertainment

- Eating out

- Taking care of a car (if you have one); car payments, etc.

- Health insurance (if you're not covered by your job)

- Any medical expenses that aren't covered by insurance

- Promoting yourself as an actor

In other cities—Chicago, San Francisco, Seattle, or Denver—the costs will be lower than in New York or Los Angeles, but not much. And remember: Taxes will take out around one-fourth of the money you make.

If you're pursuing an acting career, you'll be spending money on these things, too:

Photography session	$300 and up
Copies of your photo	$100 per 100 copies
Résumé copying	$10 per 100 copies
Photo postcards	$50 per 100
Postage	$20 and more every month
Classes (acting, voice, movement)	$25 or more per class
Reading (books, newspapers, scripts)	$20 or more a month

As you can see, the need for money quickly adds up!

And when you're ready to join one of the unions, the fee will be close to $1,000. After that you'll pay dues of $35 to $50 a year.

These numbers aren't meant to scare you or make you give up acting. You just need to know ahead of time how important it will be to have enough money to live comfortably while pursuing a career. It does not need to be difficult. For instance, if you're earning close to $100 a night from restaurant work, you'll have enough for your monthly needs in about fifteen working days (even enough to pay your taxes). After that, the money you earn can go toward your career.

The important thing is to know that you'll need to support yourself for months or years as you begin your acting career. So find some kind of work that you'll enjoy.

HAVE FUN WITH YOUR LIFE, TOO

It's not easy to work on your career or do anything well if you're always worried about paying the rent or eating. You need to find a way to make enough money so that you can enjoy your life. You may need to give up some things you like so you can be an actor, but if you have to do this for many, many years, it's easy to get depressed. That can make pursuing your career even harder. Find a way to make enough money so that you're not feeling needy.

Your hopes for enjoyment should not be tied up in your acting career only. Find some time to do other things you enjoy, to be with friends, and to develop your life in other ways. If you base all your hopes on your acting career, but don't reach the success you wanted, you may feel bad about life or disappointed in yourself. It's very difficult to be a professional actor, so you need other activities in your life—and other people besides actors. Those other sources of joy will keep you feeling good and give you energy as you go.

The same can be said of any career you might choose: The more things you have in your life outside your work that you enjoy, the happier and more successful you're likely to be.

TALKING ABOUT ACTING

I asked a young friend who acts: Do you think you'll be a professional actor?

Megan, age 12: *I probably will do something with entertaining people, because I don't think I can picture myself doing anything but that. But I don't want to starve, either.*

Does this sound like she's starting to tell herself before she even begins that she will *not* have what she wants? When it comes to money, it's good to have your eyes open to reality. But if you say your only choices are: *"I can do what I want and be poor,"* or *"I can do something I don't like and not be poor"*—then you're twisting things around. The truth is, you *can* be an actor and have money.

Networking

IT'S OFTEN SAID IN SHOW BUSINESS that it's not what you know, but *who* you know that makes the difference between minor and major success. This is true in any business, but very important in an acting career. Many people who are stars today are related to, or have close connections to, other actors, agents, directors, producers, or others.

This means that show business is not really fair. But it's natural for people to feel more comfortable working with someone they know than getting to know someone new. There might be two actors a director thinks are right for a role. But if he liked working with one of them a lot, he will probably cast that actor.

Networking is the term used to describe people's system of getting to know each other for the sake of their careers. You want to talk to other people in your career field and find out what they do. If you can get another person to be aware of you, that person may tell others about you, or tell you about people they have met. As a result, you make links to a number of other people in your profession—people you might never have met, and who might be able to assist you. Over time, the links keep growing, and you have your own little network.

Let's see how an actor networks with others in the business.

BE YOURSELF

Young actors starting out often try to be someone they are not, striving to make a good impression on others. Acting is a business based on performing and acting, so some actors think they have to play a character even when they're at a party or meeting others. But networking is really about making honest connections. You really want to know people on the basis of a shared love for performing. If you're being phony, or trying to be someone other than who you are, most people will notice. They may not be interested in getting to know you further or working with you.

You probably have noticed a phony attitude in someone you know at school. You can tell that person is straining to create a look, or is stretching the truth. Ever notice how difficult it can be to have a conversation with him or her? Well, professional show business people will know if you're putting on an act, so it's best to be yourself. Just aim to be the best self you can be.

It can be hard sometimes to be yourself. We all have doubts and fears about who we are. Though you want to be confident in your skills and about yourself, it's not possible to feel strong and happy all the time. But one of the ways we connect with other people is through our ability to feel all kinds of emotions. When you're networking to pursue your career, it's easy to forget about the human side of the relationships. You don't want to see people only as a way to get what you want. Nobody you'll meet wants to be treated as just another stepping stone to your success.

The performing arts are based on our feelings, hopes, and beliefs, so your relationships with other people in the business need to be based on your shared human qualities. You might be feeling nervous at an audition, but a casting person might also be feeling nervous that he or she won't be able to find actors who will please the director.

Agents and casting people are human, just like everyone you've

TALKING ABOUT ACTING

I asked one young actor: What do you think it would be like to be a professional actor?

Ned, age 15: *It would be tough looking for new work! You have to look through the paper every time you're not doing something. And going someplace new, like New York, where you're not known at all—it seems like it would be really tough. Everyone else is as good as you are, if not better. And they already have experience there.*

Yes, as a newcomer, you have to work twice as hard just to get noticed. When you move to a new place, it's best to build your career one step at a time. If you expect to be an overnight success, you'll probably get so disappointed it will be harder to do the work you need to do. So don't expect to get your first job right away. In the beginning, take classes and get to know people.

always known. So make your links with people from your heart and soul.

HOW TO NETWORK

The best way to begin learning how to network is right in your own area. You should start out with local theater activities. Read the arts section of the newspaper for a while to find out which theaters put on shows and what kinds of shows these are. Does one director's or actor's name keep popping up in the articles you read? That person might be a good person to talk to. As a way to practice, the next time you see that person's name, try to go see the show he or she is connected with. If you liked the show, go backstage and tell that person.

This can take courage. But remember this: Actors and other show business people love to hear what you liked about their work. He or she will probably be delighted to hear your comments. This is not a time to be pushy, or to ask if any jobs are coming up. This is simply your first meeting. The next time you see that person's name in the news, go see his or her latest show, and begin to develop that first contact into a friendship if you can.

If you read the theater publications, or "trades," as often as you can, some names will become familiar. After a while, if you go to audition for a play that's being directed by Don Jonas, you'll know from reading the trades what Mr. Jonas has directed in the last year. If you can talk with him for a minute or two about the play or the production, you've entered into the world that he knows. You've made a contact.

Another thing to remember is that it can take years and years for some of these first contacts to grow into a chance that you'll be working together. At times, an actor makes such a strong impression that a director or casting person will think of him or her for a certain role that's coming up. But you must be prepared to continue your networking for many months or years.

If you're going to an audition for a play or film, try to find out who the director is. Then go to the library and find out what he or she has done recently. See the film or read the play (perhaps there is also a review of the play you can read). You'll have an instant conversation-starter.

Once you've made the first contact, ask if you can keep in touch with the person. You can send a photo and résumé to start, then follow up with a photo postcard in a few weeks, or a flyer for a show that you're in.

(You'll read more about sending out stuff on pages 99–101.)

Whenever you get a new photo and do a new résumé, send them. Send a greeting card!

But bear in mind that many other actors contact directors and other people in the business as well. You'll probably need to keep in touch for a long time. If you can find a way to make your mailings stand out from the others—but without getting weird—try that.

You'll also need a method to keep track of the people you're contacting. Computers are very handy for this. You can put the name of a new person into a database, then prepare your mailing. If you don't have a computer, you can keep the information on paper, with a list that includes:

• The name of the person you contacted

• The date you sent the person information

• What you sent (photo, flyer, etc.)

A NETWORKING ACTOR

Let's follow Mark, the actor from "A Day in the Life" (page 20), as he networks his way into a role. Mark has decided to take an acting class with a teacher in New York that he's heard good things about. After several weeks, he finds out that one of the other actors in the class, Alan, is appearing in an off-Broadway show. He likes the work Alan does in the class, so he goes to see the show. Afterward, he goes backstage to tell Alan how much he enjoyed the performance.

The next week in class Mark asks Alan if he would do a scene with him. Alan says yes. They begin work on a scene, and a few days later Alan says he's auditioning for a new show. He invites Mark to come along.

At the audition, Alan introduces Mark to the director, who knows Alan. Mark does a good job of reading from the script. The director likes Mark's audition, but he doesn't have a role for him in this show. Still, he calls another director who does need an actor to fill a role—one that a cast member had to give up because of the flu. The second director calls Mark in for a brief audition and casts Mark on the spot!

Mark has to work hard because the show opens in a week. But his training helps him get ready and act the role well.

You can see from this example how each person you meet may introduce you to other people, who may tell others about you, and so on. That's networking.

So keep a list of people whose work you enjoy and respect, and try to keep up on what they're doing. A large part of networking is keeping track of what's going on in your field. Networking is a desirable skill to have in *any* field you work in. Learn how to do it well early in your life, and you'll get ahead.

Overcoming
Your Doubts

ONE OF THE MOST IMPORTANT TRAITS a successful actor has is *confidence.* People who get onstage and speak in front of other people have found a way to feel they can do the job and do it well. But to get those jobs, actors have to go through audition after audition. They are turned down so many times for roles that they can form serious doubts about what they're doing. To keep going they must build a great deal of confidence in themselves. Let's look at some ways to do this.

CONFIDENCE IN YOUR ACTING

To gain the confidence you'll need as a professional actor, you want to make sure you have two things: *Good training,* so that you're sure you know what you're doing, and *experience* in the performing arts. Two or three years of training and another two or three years of experience are the least you'll need in order to feel comfortable working on a new role. Four or five years of training and the same amount of experience are even better.

When you are cast in a role, your experience will have shown you what the process of rehearsal and performance is like. Going into rehearsal for a new show or film is complex. You must get to know the director and the other actors and learn how to work well with them. You must figure out what style the play will have. So you don't want to feel unsure of what you need to do in order to play your role. You want to be

The more experience you have acting in different kinds of roles, the more confidence and creativity you can bring to your acting.

free to create a character who makes sense within the story the play is telling.

Occasionally, a young actor who has little training will get a lucky break and get a major role in a play or film. Sometimes that actor can get by on his or her personality and good looks for a while. That actor probably just appears confident and seems to be headed for success. Those are nice traits to start out with, but without the training and experience to know how to create an exciting role time after time, he or she won't be a success for long.

The other way to gain confidence through your acting is to discipline yourself to work. Working on a monologue to do at auditions, on a character you've been cast to play, or on improving your skills, the more you work on your acting, the more confidence you'll have.

If the audition or opening night arrives and you're not quite sure of your lines, you're adding fear of making a mistake to the nerves that normally occur at these times. But if you know your lines very well, and you're very comfortable in the character's shoes, you'll easily transform the audition or play into an experience of success. Taking the time to do the work well will also strengthen your reputation as a professional.

CONFIDENCE IN YOURSELF

Whether or not anyone has told you that you're a unique and wonderful person, you are. No one else can see things through your eyes. No one else has had exactly the same experiences and thoughts as you have. Each one of us has talents and gifts to give to the world, and you do, too.

Confidence comes from knowing that no matter what you do, or whether you succeed or fail at anything, you still have worth and importance.

Sometimes parents get so busy they forget to teach you to feel good about yourself. Some parents can make you feel bad even though you get good grades and behave well. Some families never learn how to give each other confidence. Some families just have problems.

Every human being on this planet matters. The best thing you can do is trust that you were born for a specific purpose and have something special to give. Then look for ways to live out that purpose. If you ever feel unhappy for a long time, talk to someone who can truly help you. Life is not meant to be a sad journey through a maze of work and difficulty. There are ways to get back or to build your confidence in your abilities and yourself.

CONFIDENCE IN THE BUSINESS

Confidence in the business comes from knowing how it works. For example, actors feel more sure about what they're doing when they know something about the people they'll audition for. If you're at an interview with an agent, and you can talk about work you enjoyed by one of the agent's successful clients, you'll show him or her that you really know what's going on in the business. Knowing who does the casting for this or that theater, you'll know where to send your photo to ask for an audition when a role comes up that you're right for.

In other words, knowledge will make you feel confident you can do things to increase your chances of success.

I have mentioned that you'll be turned down for roles—it's a fact of life

TALKING ABOUT ACTING

I asked one young actor I know: What part of acting is hardest for you?

Ollie, age 12: *I'm better performing in front of an audience that I don't know at all than I am in front of my parents and relatives. I'm afraid I might let them down if I mess up.*

A lot of actors feel this way. Yet the people closest to you are the ones who know that even if you make a mistake you're still the same person they care for. The more you can focus on enjoying the work, and the better prepared you are, the less likely it is you'll make a mistake or feel bad if you do.

for actors. Confidence means that you'll understand that rejection is just a part of the business you're in. It is not a rejection of who you are. That's one of the most important things actors must learn about the way show business operates.

You may have to audition many, many times over the course of many years before you begin to be a successful working actor, but you must not take the rejection personally. This means that if you're not chosen for a role, it probably has nothing to do with your talent or skill. Perhaps the actor who was chosen already knows the director. Perhaps the choice was based on whether the actor has an accent, or because of the rhythms of his or her speech. Most of the time, you won't have any idea why someone else was chosen. The best thing is just to trust that when the time is right, it will happen for you.

Whether or not someone has helped you learn to believe in yourself, confidence is a quality that will help you greatly when you're turned down. Be confident, and remind yourself after every audition that you're special, whether or not you get the part.

There are plenty of old sayings you can repeat to yourself, if that helps:

- "That's the way the cookie crumbles!"

- "That's life!"

- "Que sera sera!" (Whatever will be, will be!)

You don't have any control over whether or not you get cast. But you do have a lot of control over how you respond to things. The healthy response is to say to yourself, "Oh, well," forget about that audition, and do your best at the next one.

If you begin to doubt yourself, it's important to overcome the doubts right away. Remember that who you are as a person and the things you do control in your life are much more important than whether you got that role. You want to have activities and friendships outside your acting life as well as within it. When you're a well-rounded person with interests of all kinds, you'll be more confident, and you'll be a better performer. Happier with your life in general, you'll feel more positive about succeeding in your acting career.

Photos

PHOTOGRAPHS ARE MAJOR TOOLS in the actor's task of furthering his or her career. If you've been to a theater, you may have noticed photos of the cast on the bulletin board in the lobby. These are a type of photo called **headshots**—and you'll need one of yourself to promote yourself as an actor.

In some smaller towns, you may be able to get started with a good snapshot picture. But offering a Polaroid-type photo to a casting director or agent will mark you as a beginner. So it's best to get a set of the 8 by 10–inch black-and-white headshots as soon as you can.

A session with a photographer will cost at least $300, depending on how many shots he or she takes. (The quality of the shots will also affect the cost.) The session will take anywhere from one to three hours. The photographer may shoot one roll of film containing 36 shots, but it may take you a while to relax. You'll probably want to have the photographer shoot at least another roll.

Headshot: An actor's headshot measures 8 by 10 inches and normally includes his or her head and shoulders in a black-and-white photo. In recent years, "three-quarter" photos have become common. These show the actor's face and body down to about the hips or knees.

As a young actor starting out, you'll probably need to get new headshots every year or so, since you're still growing and changing. Later, every two to three years will be all right as long as your look remains about the same. But if you change your hairstyle or have cosmetic surgery, you'll want new photos. After all, you want to look just like the person in your headshot when you walk into an audition.

TYPES OF HEADSHOTS

Many professional actors get headshots for three different purposes: one for commercials, one for theater, and one for film. At some point early in your career, you'll probably want to have three rolls of shots taken by your photographer—one roll for each type of headshot.

You'd probably want to wear casual clothes for a commercial shot, and the photographer would probably suggest relaxed body positions. Remember that agents and casting directors look for a certain energy in a headshot. Most commercial shots are "smile" shots: The actor is smiling and his or her eyes show energy. These are good shots to do at the beginning of a session when you're fresh and lively. They're difficult to pull off if you're a little tired.

Headshots for theater and film are usually more serious-looking. The photographer may suggest dark clothing or a more dramatic style of dressing. This is where you can really "show your stuff." Be sure to let your eyes reflect energy again—and the depth that you feel inside.

FINDING A PHOTOGRAPHER

There may be someone in your hometown who does actors' headshots, but make sure that person takes black-and-white photos for *actors.* You do not want a "portrait"–style photo. There can be big differences in style and approach between headshots and portraits.

If you live in a large city and have the opportunity to choose from several photographers, arrange to meet about three of them. Look at the work they've done for others and think about how you'd feel working with each. Just as you get along better with some friends than with others, you'll probably find you're more comfortable with one photographer than with another. Each has a unique style: You can tell by looking at their work whether or not you like their approach.

When you first talk with the photographer, ask him or her to make some suggestions about your "look." As you learned on page 4, most people in the business categorize actors in their files into types: a young mom or dad, a young romantic lead, a business person, and so on. The photographer will have some ideas on this, so ask about type.

Photo by Nick Granito

In the standard headshot, like Chris O'Connor's, a natural smile is always a good bet. Notice that Chris has had his name printed at the bottom of the photo.

CHRIS O'CONNOR

Photo by Steve Kida

TANYA OESTERLING

Tanya Oesterling's photo is a good example of a three-quarter shot.

Also ask about what kinds of clothing you should bring to the photo session. You should plan to dress neatly and comfortably in a way that makes you feel like yourself, for your photos as well as your auditions. Casting directors and agents do expect the actors they do business with to look professional, so it's not a good idea to wear jeans with holes in them or other sloppy clothes as part of your "look."

THE NATURAL YOU

Even though the world of acting appears to be full of glamour and mystery, most agents and casting directors prefer to see a *natural* look in an actor's headshot. It's important to look your best in the photo, but you want to look the way you do on any day you're enjoying life and feeling great—not as if you're getting all done up to go to the Academy Awards. (Even the stars would find it a lot of trouble to dress for the Academy Awards every day.) Most people in the business prefer a fresh, relaxed look in photos. If they need to make you more glamorous for a role, they'll hire hair and makeup professionals.

Many actors use makeup for their photo sessions because the camera picks up every flaw. Your photographer will probably be able to suggest a makeup person for you to work with. Black-and-white photography requires a special knowledge of makeup colors and techniques. So unless you're very experienced, you shouldn't do your own makeup for your photos.

If you study the work of the photographers you visit, you'll be able to see which ones achieve a natural look *with* makeup in their photos. A good makeup artist can bring your face alive on film, but without giving you a "made-up" look. Be sure to tell the makeup person that you want a *natural* look rather than a *glam* look. Remember, you need to look just like your photo; otherwise the agent or casting director may become confused about who you are.

....

TALKING ABOUT ACTING

I asked one young actor: What do you want from an acting career?

Paula, age 17: *I want success, not in the form of money, but in the form of really great parts. I want it to get even better than I thought it would get.*

Sounds a bit like you need to come back down to earth! It's good not to see success only as making money, but few actors win those great parts. Successful actors must work hard, audition, and network, even for small roles. The chances to do the great parts are rare. If you start out as too much of a dreamer, you may give up many things in life for something that might not happen. Then you could feel that life is not "better than you thought it would get," but a "bummer."

CONTACT SHEETS

A few days after the photo session, you'll be able to look at *contact sheets* of your photos. These are groups of very small versions of the shots that were taken. It may seem odd to have so many images of yourself staring back at you. It helps to cut a square out of a piece of paper, about the size of one of the prints, so that you can cover up the remaining images while you look at each one. The images you choose will each be blown up into an 8 by 10–inch picture. You'll go to a photo duplicating service to have more copies made.

As you study the contact sheets, look for a photo in which you look relaxed and energetic. As you've learned, an actor's photo should project a lively quality without overwhelming the viewer. Look for one where your eyes sparkle, where you look like you live life fully. If you choose a shot where you're smiling, make sure the smile looks natural and not forced. Check to make sure there are no funny shadows on your face, or distracting elements in the background.

The photographer can help you choose a good photo, and if you know any professional actors, they may give some advice as well. If you're on good terms with others in show business, like an agent, a director, or a casting person, ask them, too. You may choose a shot based on their advice, but be sure that *you* like the shot, too. You should like the way you look in it, because you'll be using the photo in a lot of different situations for a long time.

COSTS

Photos are one of the biggest investments actors make in their careers. Besides the cost of the photographer, you'll need to spend between $50 and $250 to have copies of your headshots made (depending on how many you start with). There are companies that specialize in making these copies, and they will charge you less than a regular film developer or camera shop. You can ask your photographer about photo duplicating services.

Questions About Promoting Yourself

IF YOU PLAN TO HAVE AN ACTING CAREER, you'll need to promote yourself using those headshots you read about in the last chapter. (You'll also need a résumé—that's the topic of the next chapter.) This chapter tries to answer six questions that are asked over and over again by young actors starting out:

1. How do I get my photo to agents and casting directors?

2. How often should I contact agents and casting directors?

3. Should I take classes with a casting director or agent so that I can meet them?

4. What do I do if I try and try, and nothing happens?

5. How can I find out what my "look" or "type" is?

6. How long should I expect building my career to take?

These questions may not sound like matters that your favorite actors would need to think about. But at one time even the biggest stars needed to answer them.

1 HOW DO I GET MY PHOTO TO AGENTS AND CASTING DIRECTORS?

There are two ways to do this. The first is to mail the photo with a résumé and cover letter.

When you mail a photo, you can follow up with a phone call to the agent or casting director, asking if you might set up a time to come in and interview. The person may be brief with you on the phone, or even rude. Many agents and casting directors prefer to make the first personal contact themselves after they've received an actor's photo. If people seem unkind, remember that it's not because of who you are, or what you want. You may have just caught them at a very busy time, or they may just be rude people!

The second way to get your photo to agents and casting directors is to drop it off at the agent's or casting director's office. Some actors in large cities such as New York and Los Angeles make contacts this way. But it's very rare that you'll get an interview or audition when you stop by to drop off your photo. Some agents and casting directors do not want actors showing up at their offices without an invitation. You may want to meet the people who could help you with your career, but they may feel that a total stranger is trying to pressure them if you just walk in.

If you did decide to go in, you'd want to respect the wishes of the person you visit. If it seems like he or she is in a hurry, just say "Thank you," and leave. Don't try to chat with someone who doesn't seem to want to talk. Don't give someone a reason to remember you in a negative way rather than a positive way.

2 HOW OFTEN SHOULD I CONTACT AGENTS AND CASTING DIRECTORS?

Once your photo is in their hands, add their name to your **mailing list.**

Using today's computer software, you can have labels for your cards and flyers printed from your mailing list. This can make it easier to do your "follow-ups" on a regular basis—about every six weeks or so. Many actors send out postcard-sized versions of their headshots that they have printed by their photo duplicating service. These handy small photos are ideal for staying in touch in a simple way. They have the actor's name and phone number and some space for a message (and a stamp) on the back.

Mailing list: When you start out as an actor, figure out a way to keep track of the people you meet and send photos to. Your mailing list should include everyone in the business you've had contact with (see "Networking," page 76).

When you're acting in a show, a film, or a commercial, you will help your career along if you send photo postcards to the business people on your mailing list. Be sure to send the information about what you're doing on the reverse side. This is a good way to keep people up to date on how your career is going, and what kinds of roles you're doing. There's always a chance someone will see and take notice of your performance if they have been told about it first. It will also help people see that you are a professional and that you pursue your work seriously.

Also, when you're in a show, you can send a flyer listing the dates, times, and place of performances. If you get a role in a film, send information about the opening of the film and where it will play.

Keep all follow-up messages short, and write clearly! Most agents and casting directors hear from hundreds of actors every week and don't have time to read long notes or messy writing.

Most actors have to keep contacting and sending messages for months or years before agents and casting directors finally call them. It's your job to keep in touch with *them*. If they don't reply over a long period of time, you may want to contact a different group of people, or change your approach.

3 SHOULD I TAKE CLASSES WITH CASTING DIRECTORS OR AGENTS SO THAT I CAN MEET THEM?

There are classes and workshops held by casting directors or agents that are also called "paid auditions." Some actors believe they're a waste of time and money. Other actors have gotten work because of the contacts they made through one of them.

Some of the people who lead these workshops do it *only for money*. There are others who truly care about helping actors. They see the workshops as a way to meet new talent. A smart actor will ask around to find out if some workshops are better than others.

You can learn a lot about show business, and sometimes about your own type, or get marketing ideas, by attending one of these workshops. If you're curious, try one or two to get a feeling for it. Maybe you'll like the way things turn out.

If you've had a particular agent or casting director on your mailing list for a long time, it might be worth it to take that person's workshop. Then he or she can meet you in person.

4 WHAT DO I DO IF I TRY AND TRY, AND NOTHING HAPPENS?

Remember that it may not be a failure in the way you're promoting yourself or anything else. Don't take the lack of response as a rejection of *you*.

Think about whether you might make some calls to people you've contacted before. Some people need a reminder before they'll agree to see you. It also might help to look at things with a fresh eye. Ask someone you trust for advice. Take a new class. Or get involved in another field in show business—lighting and sound for the stage, camera work for the screen. The more you can learn, the better off you'll be.

It's hard to understand sometimes why some actors are successful and others are not. There may be no reason that anyone can see. Some actors pursue a career for a long time without getting the work they wanted. They decide they're not getting as much out of it as they're putting in. At some point, then, they do think about leaving the business. They may quit acting, or simply quit trying to make a living at it. They may then act in small theaters, just to enjoy it.

Also, the acting business seems to worship youth and beauty. Actors don't stay young forever, and not everyone is gorgeous. This can make it hard to keep a career going.

But you can always find a place to use your acting talent. Most places you act will not have the pressure that the large cities have.

If you become an actor and then feel unhappy with the way your career is going, you can take some time to make a decision. You may stop acting for a while, or continue

....
TALKING ABOUT ACTING

I asked a young actor friend: What do you think it would be like to be a star?

Quentin, age 14: *I really wouldn't want to be a star. I'd like people to know who I am, but not to the extent of not being able to walk down my own street without people saying, "Oh, look! It's so-and-so!"*

It's easy to see why you feel that way. The lives of stars seem full of stress and trouble. Many have to hide from reporters, or hide from public view. If you don't want to be a star, how would you behave in this profession where stardom *does* happen to people? It might appear to others that you are sending the message, "I don't really want this"—even at auditions. You might not do your best work. So you must be open to whatever may happen, or make choices such as not auditioning for a starring role—if you don't want to be a star. It's best to know clearly what you want.

pursuing a career. Whatever you choose to do, you want to make sure that you're enjoying some part of your life. You want to have activities and friends outside the acting business. You just can't know ahead of time if you'll be successful. If you don't reach your goal, it will be much easier if you've at least enjoyed the ride.

5 HOW CAN I FIND OUT WHAT MY "LOOK" OR "TYPE" IS?

One way is to go to as much theater as you can and spend some time watching commercials and television shows. Compare the types of people you see with how you look yourself. You'll get a general idea of where you might fit in. Another resource is a book called *The Player's Guide,* which you may find in major libraries and at offices of the actors' unions. This guide lists actors and actresses *by type.* It is sometimes used by casting directors to cast specific roles. It can help educate you about particular looks and types.

6 HOW LONG SHOULD I EXPECT IT TO TAKE TO BUILD MY CAREER?

In some cases, actors have begun to work steadily after pursuing a career for only a few years. But most can expect to work on their careers for ten to twenty years before making a living at it. In many cases, actors promote themselves well and make a living doing what they enjoy. But they never find the great success, fame, or money they hoped for. The reasons are usually unknown. It may not be a lack of talent. It may just be timing or luck, or any of a number of reasons. As most actors know, there are many, many talented actors who don't work a lot.

Résumés

The résumé is one of the actor's most important tools for promoting his or her career. A résumé lists the actor's work experience and other information that would interest anyone who would consider him or her for a role. (See the example on page 97). This includes the actor's height, weight, and hair and eye color, and also such things as the range of his or her singing voice and special skills. Let's look at how you can prepare a professional-looking résumé to get your own career off the ground.

Your résumé should be printed on an 8 by 10–inch sheet of paper. Of course, it must be typed. Casting people usually look at a résumé for only a few seconds, so you need to keep your résumé on one page and be sure it's clear and easy to read. A confusing or crowded-looking résumé will turn people off, so never try to squeeze too much information onto it. As you get more skills and new and better credits, you simply remove the old ones, rather than making the type smaller or more jammed together.

THE FORM OF A RÉSUMÉ

First of all, your name and telephone number must be at the top, either in the center or on the left margin, as the example shows. It's better not to include your address, because résumés can fall into the hands of people who are up to no good. You never want to advertise where you live.

Many actors pay for an *answering service* that will take their calls for

ELIZABETH WETMORE

(555) 555-9775
Fax: (555) 555-9593

Height: 5'10"
Weight: 140
Hair: Brown
Eyes: Hazel
Voice: Second soprano/alto

PERFORMANCE

THE HEIDI CHRONICLES	Heidi	Walnut Hill Theater Department, Natick, Mass.
BRIGHTON BEACH MEMOIRS	Nora	Walnut Hill Theater Department
THE WINTER'S TALE	Emilia	Walnut Hill Theater Department
A CHORUS LINE	Ensemble	Walnut Hill Theater Department
PHOENIX	Wendy Star	Walnut Hill Student Theater
MUCH ADO ABOUT NOTHING	Beatrice	Hartsbrook Theater Dept., Hadley, Mass.

TELEVISION

BIODIVERSITY: WILD ABOUT LIFE!	Ariel	Video for WGBH, Boston
SMOKESCREENERS	Sisko	Video for Arnold Advertising and CF Video, Watertown, Mass.

EDUCATION & TRAINING

Walnut Hill School for the Arts, Natick, Mass. (*Cum laude* graduate with major in theater; recipient of Theater Performance Award)

Acting:	Christopher Cull, Joseph Cabral
Voice:	Mary Chestnut
Dance:	2 years ballet; 3 years jazz; 1 year tap
Movement/dance:	Kirsten McKinney

SPECIAL SKILLS

Dialects:	British, American, French (also fluent)
Musical instruments:	Recorder (tenor, alto, and soprano)
Other skills:	Horseback riding; bicycling; roller-skating; swimming; diving; yoga; knitting; embroidering; typing; American Sign Language

them. The answering service telephone number is the one they list, not their personal number, so that people won't be calling them at home. If you can, you should get an answering service also, for the same reason. If you're working with an agent, it's best to list the name of the agency and its phone number, rather than your own.

Under your name and service phone number, list your height, weight (if you want to), hair and eye color, and your **vocal range** if you are a singer. Below this, put in your experience—or *credits*—for theater, film, and television, in three separate sections. If you're in New York, list your theater credits first; if you're in Los Angeles, list your film credits first. Include the name of the show, the role you played, and the theater at which it was performed. In the case of film and TV, the name of the director or the television network goes in place of the theater name. In the example, the actor has no film experience, so she simply lists her theater and TV credits.

Vocal range: This refers to the type of voice you have: bass, baritone, tenor, alto, mezzo-soprano, or soprano. You can find out from a voice teacher, vocal coach, or choir director what type of voice you have. Provide your range on your résumé only if you sing well—casting directors may call you to audition for singing roles.

Actors who have done commercials want to include that experience on their résumés. They should have a copy of the commercial on videotape, and then state on the résumé: "Videotape available on request."

If you've only begun acting, you may be tempted to "pad" your résumé —add credits for shows you haven't actually performed in. This is a no-no! Casting people understand that everyone has to start somewhere, and it's pretty easy for them to spot a résumé that's padded. Some casting people have read résumés with phony credits for shows they had cast themselves, so they knew the résumés were false—and threw them away. An actor must build a name as a professional in the business, and that means being honest about what you've done and how you've trained. Nothing can turn off a casting person faster than knowing an actor isn't truthful.

The next section of your résumé lists your training. Here you can include your acting training and/or classes, voice training, movement or dance classes, and any other training you've gotten. If your acting teacher is fairly well-known, you may want to list his or her name—otherwise the school name is fine.

The final section of the résumé is a list of the actor's special skills.

I asked one young woman if there was any advice she'd give to other young actors.

Rhonda, age 17: *Always be looking for ways to improve your acting. Don't let yourself be average. Never think you are the best you can be—always try to get better.*

Yes, it's important to keep training yourself and improving. But be careful—don't tell yourself that you're not good enough, or that most other actors are better. Believe in yourself and your abilities *and* at the same time work to be even better.

These can be anything from doing dialects or magic acts to playing sports. Perhaps you do special character voices—such as Arnold Schwarzenegger or Donald Duck. It's important to list only skills that you can do well. If you list basketball, a casting person may call you to audition for a role because you claim that you can play basketball. You need to be able to perform in an audition "game," and be a pretty good shot, too. If you list fields of interest you know a little about but don't perform well in, you'll mislead casting people. They'll be surprised and not very pleased if they call you in to show them a skill you don't really have.

FINISHING TOUCHES

You can get your résumés copied at most printing or copy shops. If you can afford it, get them copied on a good-quality paper. Casting people slide résumés in and out of files, so they need to stand up to a lot of shuffling.

Ask for a test sample, or the first copy, and check to make sure it looks straight and centered on the page. When you have your résumé copied, ask to have the copies cut to 8 by 10 inches, to match the size of your headshot. Otherwise, you'll be stuck with the need to trim each one yourself to the size of your photo. You don't want the résumé to stick out over the edge of the headshot—it will look bad and be torn as it's moved around.

Your résumé must be stapled or glued to the back of your photo. If your photo and résumé are not connected to each other, one may get lost, and the person you give it to will have your photo with no phone number, or your résumé with no idea of what you look like.

Every time actors do a new role, they list it on their résumés. When you've had a number of roles, and your résumé begins to get crowded, remove some of the less important roles or roles done at less important theaters. Then it will be up to date and still easy to read.

Experienced performers know that the résumé is not who they are—it's just the list of their work experiences. When you look at people's business résumés, you know they have a life outside that. Your résumé

Your Name
Street Address
City, State, Zip
Telephone Number

Date

Mickie Johanson
Artists Plus Agency
1201 El Huenga Blvd.
Los Angeles, CA 99999

Dear Ms. Johanson:

I'm new to the Los Angeles area, and I'd like to introduce myself to you. I recently graduated from Northwestern University, where I performed the roles of Kate in *The Taming of the Shrew,* and Amanda in *Private Lives,* among others.

I'm currently studying with Ralph Hemson at the Studio for Actors, and we'll be presenting an evening of one-acts next month. I'd like to invite you to attend a performance. Enclosed is a flyer outlining the dates and times of the shows, along with my photo and résumé.

I'd enjoy meeting with you for an interview or audition, at your convenience. Please let me know if you'd like to attend one of the Studio performances, and I'll reserve a complimentary ticket in your name.

Thank you for your consideration.

Sincerely,

[*sign the letter here*]

Your name

Enclosure

doesn't represent the whole of who you are. So when you write your first résumé, don't give in to the feeling that you'll never do enough to impress people. Have faith that you are already an interesting person, and that you'll fill up the empty spaces on that page with good roles at good theaters as time goes by.

THE COVER LETTER

Whenever you mail out a résumé and photo to a casting director or other show-business person, it should have a **cover letter** (see page 100) attached to it. The cover letter should introduce you and explain in a simple and well-written way why you are contacting the person. Of course, the cover letter, like the résumé, must always be neatly typed, for two reasons: First, it looks much more professional. And second, some people don't want to read handwriting, even if your handwriting's terrific. Remember, too, that casting people and agents are busy, so keep the letter brief and clear.

Your cover letter doesn't have to follow the example on page 100 exactly, but this is a good guide to what one looks like. Actors who are professional always make sure they spell the name of the person they're writing to correctly. (Notice the name "Mickie"—it's an unusual spelling). People don't like to receive mail with their name spelled wrong!

Which sex is the person if his or her first name is Mickie—or Lynn or Sandy? It could be the name of a male or a female, so you'd need to find out for sure. Finally, you'd check your letter for misspelled words, make it nice to look at, and then paper-clip it to your photo and résumé and mail it off.

Self-Esteem

WE'VE ALREADY SAID HOW IMPORTANT it is for an actor to be confident. No actor wants to go on the stage or in front of a camera feeling there is something wrong with him or her. Actors need to feel sure of their abilities. But also they need to love the art of acting—not just pursue acting so they can "fake it" and get through life. They need what is called *self-esteem.*

As everyone knows, there's a big difference between truly feeling confident and pretending to be confident. Some people *appear* to be sure of themselves all the time. They never seem to make a mistake, causing others to wish they could be as "together" as that person. But their appearance can be a cover-up for other kinds of feelings—a fear of seeming foolish, or confused, or boring. In other words, feelings people have that there is something wrong with them.

Of course, this lack of self-esteem is not a healthy way to deal with others. People who pretend to be perfect are usually quite afraid of making a mistake or of doing something to offend other people. Their "air of confidence" is just a mask.

Sometimes in an acting career you may meet someone who is faking it. He or she will boast about this or that role, or talk about all the famous people he or she has worked with. But sometimes you can't tell it's a bluff. Some actors are good at making things up about their experiences and careers.

WHAT IS SELF-ESTEEM ALL ABOUT?

Actors have a lot to offer their friends, family, and the people who come to see them perform. That's what makes most actors feel good about themselves. It gives them a sense of their worth, whether they make it on Broadway, or act in a community theater in the smallest town in Iowa. That's self-esteem.

Having self-esteem doesn't mean that you have to feel sure of yourself all the time. Healthy self-esteem means that you care for yourself and believe in yourself even if you make a mistake, or fail at something you try to do. It's important for an actor to be human. That makes people want to watch you.

We've already talked about how important training is. As many actors pursue their careers, they continue to take classes of some kind in order to stay confident in their skills. This keeps their belief in themselves strong. You may not get steady work as an actor in the first few years of your career, so you'll need to find ways to keep building your self-esteem.

Another way to build confidence in your work is to focus on what you do well, rather than on things you did poorly. If you feel like you "blew it" at an audition, remember all the other auditions you felt good about. Even if you weren't cast, you did work you can be proud of—and you can do great work in the next one.

Rather than dwell on mistakes they have made, actors need to put their attention on the future. There are other auditions to come. But starting out in an acting career, it's sometimes very hard to look ahead. You may audition for a role that you've always wanted to play, but then not get cast. It's easy to feel you'll never have another chance, or that you'll never make it. Many actors have become deeply depressed about losing a role they dreamed of playing. The problem with this is that it gets in the way when they go to the next audition. Their sadness or anger shows through, and their work isn't as good as it could be. If they get stuck in their troubled feelings, the problem just gets worse.

If this happened to you, the best way out would be to see that you're just having a bad time *right now,* and that things will get better. As one actor said, "I feel so low, there's nowhere to go but up." Also, the Actor's Fund, an organization that helps actors, offers free or low-cost "crisis counseling." If you got into a depression that lasted for more than a few weeks, you could see a counselor or therapist. (If you're in any situation where someone is making you feel like you can't do anything right, you may need some help getting out of that "bad scene." The Actor's Fund and the Actors' Work Program exist to give you a hand with that.)

FEELINGS AND SELF-ESTEEM

Some people choose an acting career because it offers an opportunity to express their feelings. Having strong feelings can make us feel out of control, "out there," even naked. It can be difficult to express feelings in social or work situations. For this reason, you may feel like "saving up" all your feelings for your acting work.

Feelings are a normal part of human life, and if you find ways to express them outside your acting, and tell yourself it's okay to do this, you'll get used to sharing your feelings with others. And that's good—as you do this more and more in your day-to-day life, your self-esteem will grow. Let's think about how this works.

Our society isn't used to seeing people express feelings in everyday life. So people who have strong feelings, but don't see other people expressing them, may simply think that nobody else has feelings like theirs. They may then try to deny their feelings, or try to cover them up (or wait to express them while performing a role, if they're actors). But once someone shares feelings, he or she usually finds out that other people have just the same kinds of feelings. It's just that they're covering them up too, for the same reasons. It's best to try sharing your feelings at first with someone you really trust—a close friend or family member. As you become more comfortable with sharing your emotions, thoughts, and beliefs with others, you'll become more confident that the person you are inside is valuable and important, no matter what you feel.

PLANNING AND SETTING GOALS

Planning and goal-setting are not much fun for most people. But they're important in keeping yourself and your life on track. If you were to move to New York City in one jump, without making any plans, and without knowing anyone there, and without saving some money first, your first few weeks in the city would probably be a shock.

Such a move would be a blow to anyone's self-esteem. But if you planned your move over a period of several months, and knew exactly where you would stay, and had a plan for finding work, and had enough money to last you a while, you could make the move with *confidence*.

It works the same way with a career—any career. If you have a plan for how to build your career, you'll be more likely to succeed. If you have goals for your life, you'll be more likely to achieve what you want to. Why should you just let things happen to you, and then try to deal with them?

Setting goals is a part of planning that a lot of people have trouble with. Many young actors set goals such as "I'm going to be a star," or "I'm going to be on Broadway in five years." These are not bad goals to have, but the problem with goals like these is that you have no clear way to work toward them.

Setting a goal is the first step in making a dream come true. But you need to choose words that make it clear that you can actually achieve the goal *all by yourself*. For example:

"I will send my photo and résumé to every casting director that casts on Broadway this year. I will call each one two weeks after I send the photos and ask for an interview."

See? This way, you actually have the power to achieve your goal. So when you have finished, you can tell yourself, "I chose to do that, and I did it. I was successful."

If you choose "I'm going to be on Broadway within five years" as a goal, there are a lot of steps you can take to try to reach it. But in the end there are too many things you can't control:

- Which shows are put on. (You may not be right for any of the roles.)

- Whether or not another actor has a stronger contact with the casting person (and gets the role because of that).

- Whether the director thinks you're just the actor for the part. (He or she may want someone who is taller.)

TALKING ABOUT ACTING

I asked a beginning young actor: What are you looking for in an acting career?

Sam, age 18: *I would be doing it for the credit. A lot of people don't become that well-known, but people who are really into it know them. I'd like to have a real name in the theater community, and I'd be respected.*

This is a more realistic goal than "I want to be a star" or "I want to get rich." It's a goal you have more power to achieve. You can get solid training in a good program; work hard; and always be prepared. Others in show business will respect you. For that kind of goal, there are steps you can take to get there.

When there are many things that you can't control, you don't have the power to achieve your goal on your own without getting lucky. And you can't count on luck. It's much better for an actor's self-esteem to have some goals that he or she can be sure of achieving on their own.

It's also important to have goals in your life outside of acting. If it turns out that you're not as successful with your career as you'd like to be, it's good to know that you can succeed in other areas of your life.

An actor's life can be full of ups and downs. It's easy to feel that there's too much information to learn and work to do, so it's important to do those other things that make you feel good about yourself. Keep your self-esteem going, and make it a point every day to do one thing you do very well—cooking, making music, dancing, talking politics—whatever it may be. And remember that whatever happens, you have gifts to offer to the world. No one can take away your relationship with yourself. Believe in yourself, and others will, too.

TALKING ABOUT ACTING

I asked a high-school acting student: What do you think it would be like to be a professional actor?

Serena, age 15: *I think it would be extremely difficult. It's a high-stress occupation that pays very little, but from what I've done and heard, it's worth it.*

If acting is what you live for, if your life would be empty without it, then you'll probably want to go for it. Just don't forget that there are easier ways to get what you want: by acting in community theaters, or exploring the arts in other ways. There are many doors open to you, so don't narrow yourself to the "I have to be a star" attitude. That can cut you off from a lot of excitement in other parts of your life.

Thirty-Five Plays to Be Familiar With

CERTAIN PLAYS AND MUSICALS ARE DONE often at colleges, universities, regional and summer stock theaters, and community theaters—places where young people often explore the idea of becoming actors. If you are not yet familiar with many plays, these thirty-five titles are good ones to begin with.

Every actor needs to know about plays—a lot of different plays—by seeing them and reading them. Thirty-five may seem like a lot, but if you're serious about a career, you'll want to read plays until you're familiar with many more. Don't feel you have to know all of these plays before you become an actor. But do keep reading. For starters, spend an afternoon browsing at the library, and choose a couple that appeal to you. Choose different types of plays to read. Watch for different styles that dramatists use to tell a story and bring their characters to life.

Often, when an audition for a particular play is announced, you can get a copy of the script to read at the library or a local bookstore. Of course there are many, many more plays that are well-written and often performed; this listing is just to give you a basic grounding in different types of plays.

Remember, your goal is just to become familiar, as most actors are, with different types and styles of plays. These thirty-five plays are listed in alphabetical order, not in order of importance. Also included is a list of musicals that are often done, for those who are interested in that popular form of theater.

CLASSIC PLAYS

Antigone by Sophocles (or the modern version by Jean Anouilh)

Arsenic and Old Lace by Joseph Kesselring

As You Like It and many others by William Shakespeare

The Children's Hour by Lillian Hellman

The Crucible by Arthur Miller

The Diary of Anne Frank by Albert Hackett and Frances Goodrich

A Doll's House by Henrik Ibsen

The Glass Menagerie by Tennessee Williams

I Remember Mama by John Van Druten

The Importance of Being Earnest by Oscar Wilde

Life with Father by Howard Lindsay and Russel Crouse

The Member of the Wedding by Carson McCullers

The Miracle Worker by William Gibson

The Miser by Molière

Our Town by Thornton Wilder

PLAYS OF OUR TIME

Brighton Beach Memoirs and others by Neil Simon

Blues for Mister Charlie by James Baldwin

Crimes of the Heart by Beth Henley

The Effect of Gamma Rays on Man-in-the-Moon Marigolds   by Paul Zindel

A Hatful of Rain   by Michael V. Gazzo

The Heidi Chronicles   by Wendy Wasserstein

A Life in the Theater   by David Mamet

Moonchildren   by Michael Weller

Play It Again, Sam   by Woody Allen

All the plays above are comedies and dramas, and are most likely shelved in your library under the author's name. Musicals, which are listed next (on page 110), are shelved differently, and you would probably find them arranged by title.

There are few actors who don't have fun performing in You're a Good Man, Charlie Brown.

MUSICALS

Annie

Carousel

The Fantasticks

Fiddler on the Roof

Guys and Dolls

Gypsy

Oklahoma!

Oliver!

Peter Pan

The Sound of Music

You're a Good Man, Charlie Brown

Also, don't forget that many libraries now allow you to check out recordings and videotapes of many of these shows. So have fun reading and exploring.

Unions

for Actors

THE UNIONS THAT YOU HAVE READ ABOUT in this book are simply organizations that protect actors on the job. Most actors join at least one of the unions. All actors should respect what they do to give performers help.

There are six unions for performers:

- Actors' Equity Association (also known as AEA, or Equity) covers work in theaters.

- American Federation of Television and Radio Artists (AFTRA) covers work in television and radio.

- American Guild of Musical Artists (AGMA) members are singers, dancers, and other performers in operas, musical productions, and concerts.

- American Guild of Variety Artists (AGVA) members work in ice shows, nightclubs, theme parks, cabarets, and variety shows.

- Screen Actors Guild (SAG) covers films, TV shows, and commercials.

- Screen Extras Guild (SEG) covers background or extra players for film and TV.

Each union has its own set of requirements for becoming a member. They all require performers to pay fees to join, and yearly dues. Most of the membership fees (paid when you first join) range from $800 to $1,000. Yearly dues usually run around $25 to $50 for each union.

If you are a member of one union, your dues for a second one, if you want to join another one, will usually be reduced. Then the first union you joined becomes your "parent union."

The major role of the unions is to make sure actors are paid a fair amount for their work. That is, they protect *minimum rates* of payment to performers. They also limit the number of hours actors can be asked to work, and they aid actors who have trouble getting paid. Some unions also provide medical and dental benefits, retirement plans, casting information, and other services.

TALKING ABOUT ACTING

I asked a talented high-school actor I know: Will you be pursuing a professional career?

Uma, age 16: *If I think I'm ready for it. College will be more competitive than high school—that's the way it'll be on Broadway. So if I feel I can keep up in college, I might try New York. But if I don't think I can, I'll probably just get a day job and do community theater. Then you still get to do it, and you kind of get a name and meet lots of nice people.*

That's a good way to find out if you want to pursue a career. In high school and college you see if you're comfortable with competition and get a feel for the kinds of roles you'd get. Even if you win the best roles, it doesn't mean you'll always get good ones, or be a star later. Theater in New York and the rest of the world will be very different from your school experiences. There will be actors with more skill and experience who have been around longer than you have.

TWO MYTHS ABOUT UNIONS

Many actors think that if they can just get a union membership card, they'll be seen as professionals and have a better chance at getting cast. These ideas are both myths. First, being professional is an attitude you have. It's not a position or status that suddenly gets you to the top. Professional status is a reputation that's built over time as an actor works with a lot of people. It shows up in your behavior and includes being on time, learning your lines, not missing entrances, being prepared, and having the skills you need to do your job well.

Some casting directors and agents will take a different view of you if you have a union card. But most can tell whether your membership in the union is based on the experience and skill they expect from a union member, or whether you just paid money for the union card so you could put it on your résumé.

As to the second myth, once you join a union you'll be competing against hundreds of other actors who have already spent a lot of time and gained a lot of experience in the business. If you're a new Equity member, and you audition

Photo by Jim Gipe

Young actors find good roles in the play The Diary of Anne Frank. *For this reason it is often performed at high schools and colleges.*

for your first off-Broadway play, there will probably be actors there who have performed in many plays on and off-Broadway. Some of them will probably already know the director. Once you join a union, you are in a bigger group of very fine actors who are competing with you for roles in theater, film, and television. And if you don't know some of the directors, producers, and casting people who will audition you, you'll have a lot of new ground to cover, compared to those who have a lot of experience.

The other thing to keep in mind about unions is that once you are a member, you cannot take any jobs that are not called union jobs. For example, if you become a member of Equity, you can't work in an off-off Broadway play that has not agreed to follow union rules. If you become a member of SAG, this means you can't work in a non-union film. Every year there seem to be more and more non-union films that make it big. Once in a while an actor secretly appears in a non-union production when he or she is a union member, but this idea is looked down on in the business. It's another type of behavior that is viewed as not professional.

So, when you become a union member you can lose chances to get hired in some of the places where actors often start out. It's best to wait to join a union until you have solid experience and have been networking for a number of years.

Yet it can be helpful to join a union when the time is right. Most unions have workshops and programs which can help you build your career. For instance, AFTRA (the American Federation of Television and Radio Artists) often holds meetings with invited agents and casting directors. These kinds of meetings can give you a lot of information about what agents and casting directors are looking for and what kinds of actors they like to work with, and improve your understanding of the business. SAG (Screen Actors Guild) also has workshops for its members.

If you become a union member and go to these workshops, you'll still want solid training and experience behind you. It's not much help to meet a casting director or agent if you haven't done much acting. Except in very rare cases, people in the business will not take a risk with a newcomer. So "pay your dues"—get good training and start building a career —before you pay your dues as a union member. You'll increase your chances of success.

Next, we'll look at how you might add a videotape to your headshot and résumé as a tool for getting ahead in your acting career.

Videotapes

VIDEOTAPES ARE ANOTHER IMPORTANT TOOL that actors use to promote themselves, though a videotape is not a necessity like a photo and résumé. Actors usually wait a while before spending their money on a videotape. Once they have gained good experience working in front of a camera, then they invest in a tape that will show them at their best. Sending out a videotape that does not show you well can do more harm than good to your career.

The actor's videotape is usually a few film scenes or commercials in which you have lines or a leading role, put together into a five- to seven-minute video. If you haven't yet worked on any films or commercials in which you speak lines, you can work on a scene with another actor and tape that. But it's very important to put only your highest-quality work on your videotape. The scene should be rehearsed well, and the camera work and editing should be professional. When you send out your videotape, or give it to casting people and agents, you'll want the tape to give them the very best impression of your work, and show that you are a serious professional.

When you're starting out, you might check out student-made films—the movies made by people in film-making programs at New York University, the University of California, and other schools. Films made by junior and senior students are usually of good quality and may be fine to put on your videotape. You can find out about the auditions for student films in the weekly theater newspapers. Often the auditions are also posted on the bulletin boards of the schools. Student films can be a good way to gain experience and credits performing on film.

HOW TO PUT A VIDEOTAPE TOGETHER

Let's say you're an actor who is doing some film work and commercials. On each job, you ask the director or the casting person about how to get a copy of your work on tape. Then you look in the Yellow Pages to find out who does professional editing in your area, or call one of the unions to ask for advice on getting your tape professionally edited. It's much better if you can find an editor who has already done videotapes for actors. He or she will already know what is needed.

The editor will help you decide how to edit your scenes together so they present you well. Remember, you are promoting yourself, so you want to focus on your image—how you look and how you come across—because on a tape that is what will have the most effect on people watching it.

The editor will also help you create titles to introduce each different part of the video. Your name and phone contact should be seen at the beginning and end of the video.

Editing time in a studio can be expensive, so ahead of time, if you can, choose which scenes you want to put on tape. Also think about the order you may want to put them in. You probably love all the work that you've done, but in choosing what to put on a video, you need to get advice from other professionals in the acting business (just as you did when looking at contact sheets from your headshot photographer). It's hard to look at your own work with a cool eye, and what you may think is a great scene may not impress someone else. If you know any actors who have been in the business awhile, you might invite them to watch your scenes, and ask them which ones might be best to put on a videotape. Even better, if you know a teacher or director who might be willing to do this, ask for their help.

Once you've had the tape edited, you'll need to get copies made. You always want to have some ready to give to casting people or agents. Never send out the original—if it ever gets lost, you'd have to start all over again. The editor may be able to tell you where you can get copies made at a fair price.

Have your name and contact information printed on both the tape itself and the box it's stored in. No one should need to watch the tape just to find out whose it is. You can make your own labels on a word processor or computer and paste them on the tape and box. You can also paste one of your photo postcards on the box—that's a good example of putting a package together to promote yourself as an actor.

FILMING YOUR OWN SCENES

If you're a member of SAG or AFTRA, you may be able to use the union's services to tape your own scenes for a video. Again, you must make sure that the work you do, and the filming of the scene, look professional.

Choose a scene that allows you to express some of your range as an actor, but keep it natural as well. You may think that if you only have five to seven minutes to show your talent, you should try to squeeze every possible emotion into the scene. But simpler is better, especially on film. You want to get casting people and agents interested in seeing *more* of what you can do—not to put the tape away thinking they've seen everything you've got.

For your scene partner, choose an actor who is on your own level of skill, but is not the same type as you are. It should be someone that you enjoy working with. If you can, find a scene that has humor as well as emotion—everyone likes to laugh. And have fun with the scene, so that when people see the tape, they'll enjoy your work even more.

GETTING YOUR VIDEO TO CASTING PEOPLE AND AGENTS

Most casting people and agents do not want to get videos they never asked for, so it's not a good idea just to mail yours out to them without an invitation. You need to make a contact with someone before you send him or her your video.

When you send your photo and résumé to a casting person or agent, you can mention in your cover letter that you have a video and would be happy to drop it by or send it to them. If an agent has called you in for an interview, you can take a copy of your video along,

TALKING ABOUT ACTING

I asked: What do you want from an acting career?

Vince, age 13: *I just want a career! It would be a dream come true to be able to have a steady acting job, preferably on the stage.*

The important thing is to keep up that enthusiasm for your dream, even while you're doing the work of building a career. If you can keep reaching for the dream, and believing in it, but also understand the work it will take, your realism may help you succeed.

then ask during the interview if the agent would like to see it. He or she may ask you to leave it. That gives you the chance to call the agent in a week or two. Ask if the agent watched it and when you might pick it up. When you work with an agent, he or she may want to keep a copy of the video to show to a casting person or producer.

Keep track of your video copies the way you keep track of how many photos and résumés you have "out there." Don't let your supply get too low. If you get a chance to send or drop off a video, you want to have one ready—not make the person wait a week while you get copies made.

And keep track of who has seen your video. If you ask someone if he'd like to see your video, and he's already seen it, you'll look a little silly.

It may seem like you have to put a lot of time, energy, and money into creating a videotape. But the more professional it looks, the more likely it is that you'll be called in for an audition or interview by someone who saw your tape. Remember to update your tape—it's like updating your résumé. When you've done a few new films or commercials, have your video redone so that it presents your work as you improve as an actor.

What to Expect from a Real Career

IT CAN BE HARD TO FIGURE OUT EXACTLY what it would be like to pursue a career as an actor. Television and magazines make it look like actors are stars whose lives are just about perfect. When you try to find out what a real career is like, you hear all about how tough it is to be an actor. The truth is somewhere in between.

When you first start out, it will probably be a very exciting time for you. You'll be getting headshots and creating your résumé, and finding out about agents and casting directors. You'll be sending out your photos and résumés, going to auditions and looking for open doors. You'll be learning as much as you can about what's happening in show business. At first, you may feel like it's more than you can handle.

Most actors soon learn not to do so much that they get tired of it after a short time. You'll have lots of time to learn all the things you need to learn, so don't do so much that you get worn out at the beginning.

Bear in mind that you may have to go to twenty-five or fifty auditions before you get cast in a role. When you finish that job, you might have to go to another fifty auditions before you get the next role. So you'll spend most of the first part of your career going to auditions and interviews, and networking, promoting yourself, and looking for ways to get work as an actor.

You'll probably be working several days a week to make money, going to several auditions a week, sending out some photos and résumés every week, and perhaps going to plays and movies whenever you can. Your life will be busy, and you'll need to take care of your health: eating well (that's right, vegetables and fruits every day), and getting enough exercise and rest. This will be very important in the long run, because if you're still acting when you're forty or fifty, you may get big roles that you must be physically fit to do. If you take care of your body when you're young, you'll stay strong and energetic as you get older.

REMEMBER: IT'S A BUSINESS

Though most actors pursue careers because they love acting, you need to remember that it's a *business*. You'll be expected to have training and skill, and to do all the work that's necessary in order to get hired.

Many actors brush this point aside, thinking that if they can just get that first good role, everything will be easy from then on. Or that if they can just sign a contract with an agent, they won't have to worry anymore about getting work. But acting is a business like many others: There is a product—*you*. You are the "package" that you're selling, and you're usually the only one selling that package. And there are many, many other actors selling their own packages. You'll need to keep up on the business side of your career, or you won't have a career at all.

Even top film stars who earn millions of dollars per picture still have to interview or audition for roles. Since there are always others who want to get to the top and take their place, the competition can turn fierce. So the smart actor never expects it to get easy. It never turns into a smooth ride. As long as you're a professional actor, you will be working at the job of finding work for yourself.

The road of building your career is a long one, and you'll go more slowly than you ever thought you would. Still, you can expect to get rewards along the way. Once in a while, a director may see

TALKING ABOUT ACTING

I asked one young actor: What do you think it would be like to be a star?

Wendy, age 14: *I think that the money and the ability to get almost any part you want would compensate for all of the drawbacks.*

Most stars don't get every part they want. There is still a lot of competition between stars for good roles, especially among women, because there are usually fewer female roles. The director or producer still does the casting, and there aren't enough starring roles to go around. Even if an actor becomes a star, the problems of life don't go away. He or she usually faces a new set of problems, such as: Once you've reached the top, how do you stay there? (Or how do you deal with it if you can't?)

your work in one show and have something coming up that you're right for. He or she may then give you a call. Or you may hear from a casting director you've been sending photos and postcards and flyers to. As a result, you may get to audition for a small film. For actors who truly love acting more than anything else in the world, each role will be a reward for making that slow uphill climb.

People in show business will tell you: "If you can do anything else and be happy, do it. Acting is the toughest field there is." This isn't meant to scare you away from pursuing a career, but simply to let you know the truth. Many actors hear that only one-fifth of the union members make more than $5,000 a year (not enough to live on) and that nine-tenths of them are unemployed—and then they think, "Yes, but I'll be different!" It's a very difficult business, but it may be a bit easier if you have been fairly warned.

FAME AND FORTUNE

You can't expect to grow rich and famous. But if you are talented and lucky and hard-working enough to work your way up to where you're in demand as an actor, enjoy it! You'll notice other people who achieve what they want and then spend the rest of their lives worrying that they'll lose it.

What if they did? There would still be ways for them to enjoy life to the full. But first they would have to see that this is so.

If you achieved a lot of success as an actor, you might wish you could sit back and believe that now you've got it made. But there are a lot of stories about actors who have become stars at a young age, then turned to drink or drugs. Believe it or not, they didn't know how to deal with success. A few young actors, like River Phoenix, have died as a result of trying to ease the tension of being a star with drugs. Others have torn up their marriages and friend-

....
TALKING ABOUT ACTING

I asked one young actor I know: What advice would you give to other young actors?

Wally, age 21: *Never forget who you are! It's easy to lose yourself in a role— I've done it many times. You have to keep a grip on reality. Sometimes it's hard to come out of the fairy tale, but you have to.*

Every so often, take stock of where you are and where you're going, in every area of your life. It's easy to go so far in pursuing your career that you lose a sense of who you really are. Then it's time to step back and think about what's best for you. If you ever felt you could be losing your grip, stop and talk to someone you trust—a family member or friend. You need to love yourself whether you achieve the success you want or not. When you take care of yourself—your body, mind, and spirit—it shows in your acting and in your relationships with people in the business.

ships and ended up alone. So if you're one of the lucky ones and win success early on, find another way to deal with tension. Get your friends and family to back you up, or find someone you trust to talk to.

No matter how wonderful it can be to make it as an actor, it's not worth it to get into a panic, get hooked on drugs or gambling, wreck your car because you were drinking too much, or hurt yourself in any other way.

There are a lot of actors who are not "household names," but you see their faces in roles here and there, in the movies, in commercials, or on TV shows. Many of these actors are happy to be working on a steady basis. They don't have to deal with the loss of privacy and some of the other problems that come with being well-known.

Many actors spend years working in regional theaters (see page 5), playing several roles in one season at a theater, and then moving to a new area to work with another theater. Some of these actors, like James Cromwell (the farmer in the movie *Babe*) and Mercedes Ruehl (*The Fisher King, Lost in Yonkers*), move on to stardom after working in regional theater for years. But they never forget how regional theater gave them many happy acting experiences. Some actors make the choice to stay on this level for most of their careers. And some choose to stay in cities like Chicago or Seattle, away from the hustle and bustle of New York and Los Angeles. They may make only part of their living from acting, but that is a good life to them.

The point is that you can make choices about what you want as you go along. What you expect from acting has a lot to do with those choices. Don't just let things happen to you which force you to go this way or that.

Next, we look at some ways you may not know about to get work as an actor and help pay the bills.

EXtra
Work and
Other Jobs

Now that you know what to expect from an acting career, it's time to learn about other ways actors get work to support themselves: Extra work, print work, and industrial films.

EXTRA WORK

Extra work is a type of acting job, usually in film, where you are a background player. Most of the time, extra performers—or *extras*—don't have any lines, but are simply seated at a table in a restaurant in which a scene takes place, or walking down a street behind the lead performers as they do their scenes.

It's important to know about extra work, because it can be a good way to make money as an actor and to meet other people in the business. Some actors make most of their living from extra work. These actors are known as professional extras.

Extra work can also be a good way to get "a foot in the door" as an actor. Sometimes extras are "upgraded" on the day they do the work, which means they may be given some lines or a some important action to do in a scene. This doesn't happen often, but a few actors have gotten their start as an extra by being upgraded in this way.

On soap operas, actors who play extra roles may be hired time after time, and sometimes they'll be given a few lines. If it's less than five lines, the job is called an *under-five*. If there are more lines, the actor becomes a *day player*. If the soap's casting person likes your work as an extra, he or she may call you to audition for a larger role. For this reason, extra work can be worth doing for any actor starting out.

One thing to be careful about if you choose to promote yourself for extra work is that some actors can get known by casting people as extra performers *only*. Then, when a role comes up that they might be right for, the casting person doesn't even think of them. In his or her mind, that actor is an extra performer. This usually only happens over a long period of time, after a casting person has called an actor again and again to be an extra.

If your choice is to make money as an actor however you can, or to be a professional extra, that's fine. But if you're doing extra work while hoping to do larger roles, be careful. This is a good example of getting carried along by whatever is happening in your career and not making your own choice about whether it's what you want to do. If you were being called for a lot of extra work, and you'd really rather have larger roles, you might think about turning some of the extra work down. You could say, "No, thank you, I'm already booked"—that way, casting people wouldn't start to think of you only as an extra.

So, doing extra work can help you to make a living as an actor, but it needs to be your choice as to whether you want to do it.

PRINT WORK

Just as some actors are professional extras, some actors do *print* work to make money. Print work involves having photos of yourself taken for magazine ads and catalogues. It's the same type of work as modeling. You may have seen some faces over and over in ads. Most of the people in ads are professional models who are very attractive, but there is a market for people who have a more ordinary look.

In magazine ads, you'll see all types of people, from young mothers caring for children to older people who take vitamins. In order to be successful in print work, you do need to be fairly attractive, and it helps a lot if your looks fit into one of the types we have talked about—a father, a grandmother, a doctor, and so on. Spend some time looking at ads in magazines, and see if you can figure out where you fit in. Do you look like the college kids in the jeans ads? Or do you look like the person who suffers from those pounding headaches? You can learn a lot about your type by studying the print work you see all around you. The closer you are to a type, the better your chances will be.

Print work is usually handled through agencies, just as acting work is. If you look in the guides that list people in the business, such as the *Ross Reports,* you'll find out which agencies handle print work. You'll need a photo and résumé, just as you do as an actor, and you can contact the print agencies in the same way.

What's different about print work is that you're not actually *acting* on a **shoot**. You may play the role of a young parent or a business person, but you don't learn lines and blocking. The director will place you in certain positions to be photographed doing certain actions. But the shots will be still pictures, not movies or videotape, and this means not moving much.

Shoot: This is slang for a photography session, as well as for the process of making a film.

In print work, it's very important that you dress exactly as if you were the type of person they're looking for. If you're going to an interview for a print job where they want a business person, your look and behavior must say, "I am a businessperson," right down to the way your hair is combed. There are so many actors who have a good look for print work that you need to fit right in.

Print work is also a good way actors make part of their living. But, again, you should do it because you want to, not just because it happened to come your way. If you don't enjoy it, then you should look into other ways to support yourself, and to enjoy yourself while you're making a living.

If you're serious about print work, you'll need to get a *composite photo* done. This is a photo that shows you as several different characters, such as a doctor, an executive, a mechanic—those character types you are right for. If you liked the photographer who did your headshots, call the same one to do your composite. He or she will probably be able to help you choose some characters for the shots, and may even know where you can get a uniform or costume if you need one.

(Any time you enjoy working with someone in the business—a photographer, makeup person, director, or actor—keep that person on a list of people to stay in touch with. This is how you make your network grow. You never know when that person's skills will come in handy again.)

TALKING ABOUT ACTING

I asked one young actor: Is there anything you don't like about acting?

Xenia, age 14: *I don't like the uncertainty of acting as a career. People have to work from role to role, and that is a bit exciting, but what it really is—is scary.*

Yes, some people do see this as exciting. It's like gambling, in a way, because you're betting that you're talented or lucky enough to make it as an actor. It's normal to be scared by the risk. That's an important part of choosing whether or not to pursue a career. If you choose a career, you need to be sure it's what you want to do even if you're scared. If you're not sure, it will probably be harder to do everything you need to do to succeed.

INDUSTRIAL FILMS

Industrial films are short films or videos made for businesses (industries and companies). These are films that promote a company's products or educate its employees or clients. For instance, IBM might make a video that is shown to new employees to tell them about some of the company's policies. Or a cleaning service might make a video that teaches their workers how to use cleaning products safely.

Industrial films offer a variety of work for actors. They are usually made in just a few days—they don't take weeks or months as a television film or movie would.

What you'll need if you want to do industrial films is much the same as what you need to do print work. It helps a lot if you have the look of a business person, if that's your type. You'll need photos and résumés and some film training. (If you already have composite shots for print work, you can use them to hunt up work in industrials).

Pursuing extra work, print work, or industrial films is just another one of those choices actors make to earn money. In the next chapter, we'll talk about things you can do to help you make some of the choices you must make.

You Can Be What You Want to Be

NOW YOU HAVE A CLEAR PICTURE of what real life is like for an actor. Is an acting career what you really want for yourself?

This is really the main question and the reason you're reading this book. This may be the most important chapter in the book, for it can help you decide if you want to become a *professional* actor.

Choosing what you want to do with your life is an important decision—one you should think about over a period of months. Is an acting career the *only* thing you want, or are there other ways you'd be happy to live your life? If you choose acting as a career, would you feel like you're "losing out" on something else? Or would you feel like you lost out if you did *not* make a career of acting? Don't make up your mind right away, but give it careful thought. Let's talk about some of the issues you'll want to look at while you're deciding.

WHAT CHOICES MEAN

Choosing one thing often means accepting something you may not like that comes with it, or giving up something else that you want.

We've already talked about how hard it can be to make your living as an actor. The stress that comes with it is an important issue to think about. If you simply want to be able to act, do different roles, and be in lots of shows, you can do that. But you may want to get training for a different career in which you can make a living with less stress. Then you could do community theater in the evenings and on weekends.

But if you really want a *professional* career in which you would also act in film and on television, then you'll need to accept the stress. You'll need to put most of your time and energy into achieving your goal. And that means giving up some other things.

Many actors have given up the possibility of getting married and having a family. They devote themselves to their careers. There's nothing wrong with making this choice—for some it's just right. But when you're making your decision it's good to know about what you may have to give up—at least for a while. It's not easy to keep a partnership going smoothly or to raise children. Acting adds to the difficulty with the need to move from job to job and travel often.

You might decide to work on your career for ten years, and then ask: "Am I happy with my acting career?" Some actors do change their minds and switch to another kind of work, maybe something easier, so they don't have to give up starting a family.

EXCITEMENT AND FUN

Many young people see the way the lives of big movie stars are shown on TV and think it's a wonderful life. When an actor reaches a level of success, it can be wonderful. But some actors become sad or discouraged after trying over and over to get work for a long time. Their careers did not turn out as they expected.

You might be looking for some excitement and fun in a career. But there is usually more than one way to find what you're looking for. As an actor, you'd be playing different roles, working with important people, having pictures taken, and maybe even performing in major Hollywood movies. But if it takes fifteen or twenty years for most actors to "get there," it makes sense to try other ways to find excitement and fun. Think about what you've enjoyed doing in your life: Do you love sports, or making music, or exploring new places? There are many things to explore in life, and many ways to have fun—and hardly any of them take fifteen or twenty years. Think of one example: Today, you can use the Internet to find new jobs and ways to learn about the world.

If you do decide to become a professional actor, don't forget about all the other parts of life that can give you enjoyment.

Some actors like playing different roles and getting out of their ordinary lives to be someone else for a while. Most people have this wish, even non-actors. It's really just an urge to express yourself. There are many ways to do that besides being an actor. You can use your sense of humor in everyday life. You can go camping one weekend and dance the tango in a class the next. There are many ways to let all those different sides of yourself come out. And it's much easier to set up a camping trip or take a dance class (or whatever you enjoy) than it is to win success as an actor.

YOUR FEELINGS

Do you really want to be an actor, or simply to be able to express your feelings? One reason some people choose to become actors is that it gives them a chance to do that.

TALKING ABOUT ACTING

I asked one professional actor: What's your favorite thing about acting?

Yvonne, age 16: *The best thing about being onstage is that for a short time my imagination takes hold, and I can be so many different things that, in reality, I could never even think about.*

But you *can* be those things in reality, because they come out of your own imagination. You don't have to be acting to be clever, or strong, or smart, or whatever quality it is that you love about the character you're playing. You already have those wonderful qualities inside, whether you're acting or not.

For most of our country's history, feelings were something people kept quiet about. Today our society is more comfortable with letting people express their feelings. It's normal to have strong feelings that you want to express, such as sadness or anger or fear. It's simply part of being human.

Some people are still not comfortable with having family members express their feelings. This may be true in your family. That could lead you to believe that the only way you can express your feelings is through acting. But this does not have to lead you to choose acting as a career.

Once you are an adult, you'll be able to make friends who understand you better than your family does. You can learn to express more of your feelings and more of yourself. When you're an adult, you can make all kinds of different choices about who you want to be and how you want to live your life. You'll no longer have to live totally by the rules set up in your family.

So this matter of feelings can affect your choice about becoming a professional actor—or not. As an adult you'll have lots of chances to let out all the things that are deep within you, even feelings that seem trapped inside. Then you'll see whether you really want to be an actor, or simply to be free to pursue your own interests.

This idea may take you some time to think about. If you're confused, you might ask a teacher or school career counselor to help you understand. The important thing to remember is that you can find ways to be happy no matter what you decide to do with your life.

MAKE YOUR OWN DECISION

It's also important for you to make the decision yourself. You want to choose any career because it's something *you* want to do. Sometimes parents push kids into a field. For instance, yours might want you to be a doctor so you'll be able to help people and make a good living. But you probably won't be happy with a career based on what someone else wants. The world is full of people who followed someone else's wishes about what to do with their lives. After time goes by, they're sad or angry that they were pushed into it.

It's okay to accept advice and think about ideas that other people have to give you. But do what you want with your life. Don't let anyone talk you into something you're not sure about. Your life is yours to spend the way you choose. Make your decision with care, and pay attention as you go along. Pursue the things that make you happy, and you'll be more successful, no matter what you picked.

If you're set on being a professional actor, then go for it! Focus your heart, your mind, and your spirit on what you want! I'll be applauding for you.

TALKING ABOUT ACTING
I asked an actor: Is there any advice you'd give to young actors?

Yvette, age 21: *Just do it and have fun, and don't get too caught up in it. Because you can do whatever you want with your life.*

Zeroing
in on Books

ACTORS ARE ALWAYS READING. Books are great sources of information that can help them with their careers. And they give them inspiration to grow and improve as artists.

Here are some books on a number of topics that I would suggest you take a look at. I have marked with a star (★) the ones that are especially good for young actors.

ACTING SKILLS

★ Barker, Sarah & Harrigan, Peter. *Introduction to Performance: Beginning the Creative Process of the Actor.* Kendall-Hunt, 1994.

Barr, Tony. *Acting for the Camera.* Borgo Press, 1994.

Bates, Brian. *The Way of the Actor: A Path to Knowledge & Power.* Shambhala, 1987.

Berry, Cicely. *The Actor & the Text.* Applause, 1992.

★ Boleslavsky, Richard. *Acting: The First Six Lessons.* Routledge, Chapman & Hall, 1949.

Brebner, Ann. *Setting Free the Actor: Overcoming Creative Blocks.* Mercury House, Inc., 1990.

★ Breed & Pate. *A Beginning Actor's Companion.* Kendall-Hunt, 1993.

Caine, Michael. *Acting in Film.* Applause, 1990.

Callow, Simon. *Being an Actor.* St. Martin's, 1995.

Chaikin, Joseph. *The Presence of the Actor.* Theatre Communications, 1991.

Cole, Toby & Chinoy, Helen K. *Actors on Acting.* Crown, 1970.

Gielgud, John & Miller, John. *Acting Shakespeare.* Scribner's, 1992.

Hagen, Uta & Frankel, Haskel. *Respect for Acting.* Macmillan, 1973.

Lewis, Robert. *Advice to the Players.* Theatre Communications, 1989.

★ Morris, Eric. *Being and Doing: A Workbook for Actors.* Ermor Enter, 1990.

Olivier, Laurence. *On Acting.* Simon & Schuster, 1986.

Stanislavski, Constantin. *An Actor Prepares,* Routledge Chapman & Hall, 1989.

Stanislavski, Constantin. *Building a Character,* Routledge Chapman & Hall, 1977.

Stanislavski, Constantin. *Creating a Role,* Routledge Chapman & Hall, 1961.

AUDITIONING

Harmon, Renee. *How to Audition for Movies & TV.* Walker & Co., 1992.

Hooks, Ed. *The Audition Book.* Back Stage Books, 1996.

Hunt, Gordon. *How to Audition.* Dramatic Publishers, 1977.

Oliver, Donald. *How to Audition for the Musical Theatre.* Smith & Kraus, 1995.

See, Joan. *Acting in Commercials: A Guide to Auditioning and Performing on Camera.* Back Stage Books, 1998.

Shurtleff, Michael. *Audition: Everything an Actor Needs to Know to Get the Part.* Bantam, 1980.

Silver, Fred. *Auditioning for the Musical Theatre.* Newmarket, 1991.

THE BUSINESS OF ACTING

Adams, Brian. *Screen Acting: How to Succeed in Motion Pictures.* Lone Eagle Publishing, 1987.

Buzzell, Linda. *How to Make It in Hollywood.* HarperCollins, 1992.

★ Callan, K. *How to Sell Yourself as an Actor.* Sweden Press, 1988.

Charles, Jill, and Tom Bloom. *The Actor's Picture/Resume Book,* American Theatre Works, Dorset, Vermont.

Charles, Jill. *Directory of Theatre Training Programs.* American Theatre Works, Dorset, Vermont. Updated yearly.

Charles, Jill. *Regional Theatre Directory.* American Theatre Works, Dorset, Vermont. Updated yearly.

Charles, Jill. *Summer Theatre Directory.* American Theatre Works, Dorset, Vermont. Updated yearly.

Eaker, Sherry, ed. *The Back Stage Handbook for Performing Artists: The How-to and Who-to-Contact Reference for Actors, Singers, and Dancers.* Back Stage Books, 1995.

★ Fridell, Squire. *Acting in Television Commercials for Fun & Profit.* Crown, 1987.

Henry, Mari Lyn, and Lynne Rogers. *How to Be a Working Actor.* Back Stage Books, 1994.

Hurtes, Hettie Lynne. *The Back Stage Guide to Casting Directors: Who They Are, How They Work, What They Look for in Actors.* Back Stage Books, 1998.

Joseph, Eric. *Glam Scam: Successfully Avoiding the Casting Couch & Other Talent & Modeling Scams.* Lone Eagle Publishing, 1994.

Lewis, M. K. & Lewis, Rosemary R. *Your Film Acting Career: How to Break into the Movies & TV & Survive in Hollywood.* Gorham House, 1993.

Logan, Tom, and Paige, Marvin. *How to Act & Eat at the Same Time: The Business of Landing a Professional Acting Job.* Broadcasting Publications, 1982.

★ Mayfield, Katherine. *Smart Actors, Foolish Choices: A Self-Help Guide to Coping with the Emotional Stresses of the Business.* Back Stage Books, 1996.

Moore, Dick. *Opportunities in Acting.* NTC Pub Group, 1993.

O'Neil, Brian. *Acting as a Business: Strategies for Success.* Heinemann, 1993.

★ Padol, Brian A., and Alan Simon. *The Young Performer's Guide: How to Break into Show Business.* Betterway, 1990.

Searle, Joan. *Getting the Part: Thirty-Three Professional Casting Directors Tell You How to Get Work in Theater, Films, Commercials, & TV.* Limelight Editions, 1995.

Small, Edgar. *From Agent to Actor: An Unsentimental Education or What the Other Half Knows.* Samuel French, 1991.

Whelan, Jeremy. *The ABCs of Acting: The Art, Business, & Craft.* Grey Heron, 1990.

OTHER HELPFUL BOOKS

Armstrong, Thomas. *Seven Kinds of Smart*. Plume, 1993.

Bramson, Robert M. *Coping with Difficult People*. Anchor Doubleday, 1981.

Cameron, Julia. *The Artist's Way*. Tarcher Putnam, 1992.

James, Muriel, and John James. *Passion for Life*. Dutton, 1991.

Kabat-Zinn, Jon. *Wherever You Go, There You Are*. Hyperion, 1994.

Laut, Phil. *Money Is My Friend*. Ballantine Books, 1979.

Lehmkul, Dorothy and Dolores Cotter Lamping. *Organizing for the Creative Person*. Crown, 1993.

Lieberman, Annette, and Vicki Lindner. *Unbalanced Accounts: How Women Can Overcome Their Fear of Money*. Viking Penguin, 1987.

Maisel, Eric. *Staying Sane in the Arts*. Putnam, 1992.

Miller, Alice. *The Drama of the Gifted Child*. Basic Books, 1994.

Newman, Mildred & Bernard Berkowitz. *How to Be Your Own Best Friend*. Ballantine Books, 1971.

Proto, Louis. *Take Charge of Your Life: How Not to Be a Victim*. Thorsons Publishers, 1988.

Winter, Barbara J. *Making a Living Without a Job*. Bantam, 1993.

Index

League of Professional Theatre
    Training Programs, 66
Letterhead, 30
Lines, learning, 28, 47-48, 82
Living expenses, 73-75

Mailing list, 92, 93
Makeup, 89
Memorizing lines, 28, 47-48, 82
Monologues, 21, 22, 27-28, 37,
    69
Motivation
    for blocking, 48-49
    character's, 44
Musicals, 28, 107-10

National Association of Schools
    of Theatre, 66-67
National Foundation for
    Advancement in the Arts, 64
Networking, 76-80
New York City theaters, 2

Opening night, 54-56

Photos
    clothing and makeup for, 89
    composite, 125
    contact sheets, 90
    cost of, 85, 90
    envelopes for sending,
        29-30
    your "look," 86, 89
    postcard, 29, 37, 78-79, 92
    résumé attached to, 99
    selecting photographer, 86
    sending to agents and
        casting directors, 92
    types of headshots, 86
    updating headshots, 85-86
Physical appearance, 4, 89,
    94-95
Physical expression of
    character, 44-46
Physical training, 9-11
Player's Guide, The, 95
Plays, often produced, 107-10
Previews, theater, 2

Print work, 124-25
Professional status, 112
Projecting, 13
Promotion, 91-95
    cover letters, 30, 34
    flyers, 27, 33
    and networking, 76-80
    videotapes, 33-34, 115-18
    See also Photos; Résumés

Regional theater, 5-6, 122
Rehearsal
    actor-director relations, 51
    blocking in, 47, 48-49
    director's feedback , 50-51
    learning lines, 47-48
    tech and dress, 52-53
Rejection, 84, 103
Repertory theater, 5-6
Résumés, 22, 78-79
    cover letter, 30, 100, 101
    envelopes for sending,
        29-30
    form of, 96-99
    listing of roles, 99, 101
    padding, 98
    presentation of, 99
Ross Reports, 30, 125

Scams, 59-60
Scene study, 68
Scholarships, 64
Schools. *See* Training
Screen Actors Guild (SAG), 111,
    114, 117
Screen Extras Guild (SEG), 111
Script, reading, 42-43
Self-confidence, 83
Self-discipline, 82
Self-esteem, 102-6
Sense memory, 69
Shoot, 125
Shyness, 25
Sitcoms, 4-5
Soap operas, 4, 123-24
Stage & Screen Book Club, 30
Stage directions, 48
Summer theater, 5-6

Take, 4
Tech rehearsal, 52
Television acting
    in commercials, 4
    in sitcoms, 4-5
    in soap operas, 4, 123-24
Temporary agencies, 72-73
Theater acting, 1-2
    on Broadway, 2-3
    in dinner theater, 7
    and film acting, 3
    in musicals, 28
    in regional and summer
        theaters, 5-6
    in repertory, 6
Theater company, 59-60
Timing, 57
Training
    acting classes, 68-70
    in college, 64, 66-67
    dance, 28
    in high school, 63-64
    of inner self, 14-15
    physical, 9-11
    and self-esteem, 103
    theater schools, 66-68
    types of programs, 42
    vocal, 11-13, 28
Type casting, 4, 86, 95

Under-five, 124
Unions, actors', 51, 59, 61,
    111-14
University/Resident Theatre
    Association, 68

Videotapes, 33-34, 98, 115-18
Vocal range, 98
Vocal training, 11-13, 28
Voice of character, 45-46
Voice-overs, 7

Warm-up
    exercises, 11-13
    on opening night, 55